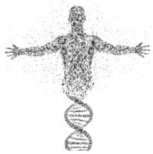

THE BLUEPRiNT
Living by the Architect's design.

Tim Cox Jr
With Matthew Elton

Foreword by Unspoken

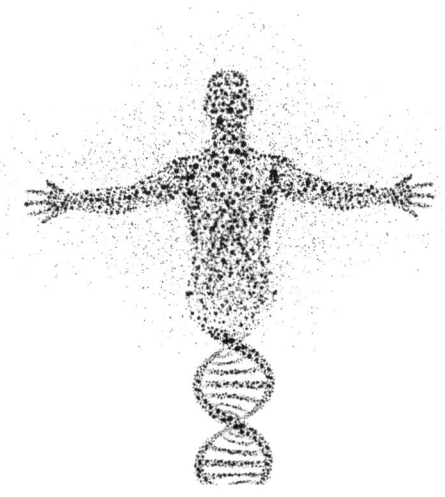

The BLUEPRiNT: Living by the Architect's design.

Copyright © 2013 Timothy Cox Jr.

All rights reserved.

First Edition. First Printing.

ISBN: 978-0-9899227-0-8

Unless otherwise indicated, all Scripture quotations are taken from the Holy Bible, New Living Translation, copyright © 1996, 2004, 2007 by Tyndale House Foundation. Used by permission of Tyndale House Publishers, Inc., Carol Stream, Illinois 60188. All rights reserved.

Printed in the U.S.A.

www.theblueprint.tv

God has put all things under the **authority** of Christ and has made him head over all things for the benefit of the church. And the church is his body; it is made **full** and **complete** by Christ, who **fills** all things everywhere with himself.
-Ephesians 1:22-23

"Every time I think of you, I give thanks to my God. Whenever I pray, I make my requests for all of you with joy, for you have been my partners in spreading the Good News about Christ from the time you first heard it until now. And I am certain that God, who began the good work within you, will continue his work until it is finally finished on the day when Christ Jesus returns. So it is right that I should feel as I do about all of you, for you have a special place in my heart..."

-Philippians 1:3-7

Dedicated to my Love City Family

To my amazing wife, Theresa.
- Always & Forever

Contents

Foreword
Unspoken Words 11

How to Use this Book
Getting the Most out of Your Journey 13

Introduction
To You the Reader 17

Chapter 1
The Unmoved Mover 27

Chapter 2
The Breath and the Barrier 45

Chapter 3
Identity 63

Chapter 4
Filled 85

Chapter 5
Showers 111

Chapter 6
Jars 131

Chapter 7
Homeland Security 157

Chapter 8
The Not-So-Sunday Church 183

Chapter 9
The Great Commission 211

Afterword
From the Author 240

UNSPOKEN Words
THE FOREWORD BY UNSPOKEN

As we travel week after week on music tours, we meet people of countless walks of life, and we realize one thing – many people have lost hope. And yes, even Christians.

In this generation, many have lost their true identities. They are dealing with pain and struggles while going through life trying to figure it all out on their own.

That's why we believe *The BLUEPRiNT: Living by the Architect's Design* is a timely reminder that we've all been created by a loving God who cares for us, knows us, and is concerned with every single aspect of our lives.

For many years, we hoped and prayed for success in our music ministry, praying for great songs and financial success. While there is nothing wrong with praying for these things, after having some of these prayers answered we've come to realize that nothing will ever satisfy us like the presence of God.

We could have 100 hit songs, hundreds of sold out shows, and the nicest tour bus, but we would still be miserable if we're not spending time with Jesus Christ. Only in Him do we find our hope and purpose, because of what He did for us that day at Calvary.

Even before we were created, God had a specific plan for each of our lives. The more we realize this, the more we can release our worries and start living according to these words of Jesus:

> *Seek the Kingdom of God above all else, and live righteously, and he will give you everything you need. So don't worry about tomorrow, for tomorrow will bring its own worries. Today's trouble is enough for today.*
>
> *Mathew 6:33-34*

In *The BLUEPRiNT: Living by the Architect's Design*, you'll find truths such as this that will make you stop and think, giving you a glimpse of God's sovereignty, majesty, and above all His infinite, unconditional love for us.

As you read through these pages we pray you'll fall more in love with Jesus than ever before. We pray you'll grow in your understanding of the loving God who created you and has a plan for you. We don't know what God's specific will for your life is, but if you surrender to His Blueprint you're sure to discover the peace and joy found only in a relationship with Him.

The dawn is breaking and I can hear Your whisper in the breeze
The world is waking and I'm here to meet You on my knees
When I'm with You my soul finds rest
Cause I can leave it in Your hands

The day keeps coming, pulling me a million different ways
I'm always running but never seem to catch the things I chase
When I'm with You my soul finds rest
Cause I can leave it in Your hands

Every sorrow, I leave it in Your hands
Every sickness, I leave it in Your hands
All my failures, I leave them in Your hands
Amen, I leave it in Your hands

So I am laying the weight of all these burdens at Your feet
No more waiting, cause You've already won my victories
In Jesus my soul finds rest
Cause I can leave it in Your hands

Every promise, I leave it in Your hands
Every healing, I leave it in Your hands
And my future, I leave it in Your hands
Amen, I can leave it in Your hands

- Unspoken, "In Your Hands"

How to Use this Book
GETTING THE MOST OUT OF YOUR JOURNEY.

The purpose of this book is to help you firmly establish nine core building blocks of a faith that is full and complete. Each chapter focuses on God's design for a specific area of your life. As each chapter builds upon the next, you will gain knowledge of God's Word and begin to actively apply it in your life. You'll experience lifechange, challenges, blessings, and joy as you learn to walk with God and build meaningful relationships with others. Your life will never be the same!

Five Key Aspects of this Book

Time: *This book is not a speed-read.* To get the most out of this book, focus on only one chapter at a time, and don't move on until you've firmly established the message of that chapter in your life. Take time to pause and reflect on what you read. At the end of each chapter is a checklist of "building blocks" to apply in your life before moving on. It may take months or even years to make full application of this book. *That's okay.* Be patient in your progress and enjoy the journey!

Bible: God's Blueprint for life is found in the pages of the Bible. This book is infused with Scripture. At the end of each chapter you'll find a list of additional Bible passages. Take the time to read these passages and reflect on their meaning, asking God to help you understand His Word.

Fellowship: Although this book can be read individually, it's ideal for one-on-one discipleship or small group study. You are encouraged to work through this book with a mentor or group of friends. Focus on one chapter at a time and meet to discuss what you've learned on a weekly or monthly basis. At the end of each chapter you'll find a list of questions to kickstart discussion, helping you build community and grow together. Please visit **www.theblueprint.tv** for free videos related to each chapter. You can watch these together, or individually and meet to discuss what you've learned.

Prayer: Be prayerful in your journey through this book. Before beginning each chapter, ask God to prepare your heart and give you wisdom. After reading each chapter, ask God to inspire and empower you to actively apply what you've learned. Pray daily for God's help in living by His Blueprint. If you're not sure what to pray, you can use the sample prayers at the end of each chapter as a starting point.

Movement: The goal of this book is **lifechange** that causes **worldchange**. As you journey through this book, you'll experience a transformation in life spiritually, mentally, emotionally, and relationally. Your story can be a powerful inspiration to others. To learn how to get actively involved in the mission of the BLUEPRiNT, visit **www.theblueprint.tv** and follow us on social media including Facebook and Twitter. Please share your progress and testimonies with us through social media by hashtagging #TheUnmovedMovement. We want to encourage and pray for you as you experience the awesome power of the Architect's plan.

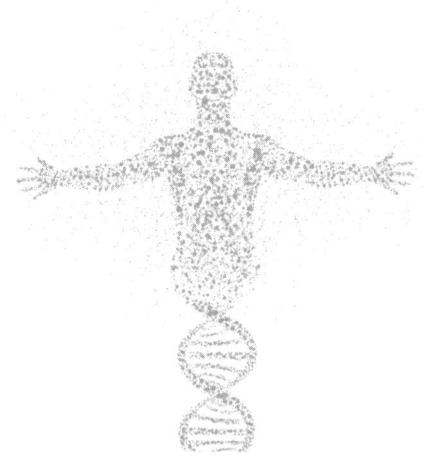

FOR FREE VIDEOS AND MINISTRY TOOLS VISIT

www.theblueprint.tv

INTRODUCTION
TO YOU THE READER

23Industries tourney to tip off at FMCC

JOHNSTOWN — The first of four 23Industries mens basketball tournaments is set to begin this evening at Fulton-Montgomery Community College.

Organizer Tim Cox Jr. has assembled 12 teams to participate in the two-day tournament. Tonight's games will be round-robin contests and Saturday will be elimination day.

Play is scheduled to begin at about 5:30 p.m. today and the players will return for a 3-point shooting contest at 10 a.m. Saturday. A slam-dunk contest will start Saturday at 5 p.m., followed by the tournament championship game at about 6

Cox started running bas

To You The Reader

Recently, my family and I got together to take a family picture at a local state campground. My mom was really passionate about capturing that perfect moment to encapsulate who we are as a family. Seven adults and seven children came together for one photo to proudly hang over the fireplace for every guest to see.

Pictures are powerful. Pictures allow us to strike a pose and present ourselves the way we want to be viewed. No matter what we're experiencing, feeling, or battling – a smile or quirky shrug can cover up a multitude of insecurities.

When you see a picture of yourself, what do you see?

What do you really see? Are you content, confident, joyous, excited, hopeful, peaceful? Only you know what the picture can't reveal – what's on the inside.

I understand this life can be exhausting. Perhaps your hopes and dreams haven't come to pass. Maybe failed relationships left you feeling lost or abandoned. Or perhaps a lack of direction or calming assurance has left you wondering whether or not you'll be able to put it all together.

You may be a single mom, an exhausted dad, or a widow. Maybe you're a ministry leader at a loss in dealing with the burdens of others' trials and hardships. You could be a mature Bible-believing Christian wondering if what your doing is what God actually wants you to be doing. Perhaps you're a brand new believer doubting your knowledge and understanding of your faith. Or you may be a non-spiritual-and-non-interested young adult feeling like God is nothing more than a crutch for the weak minded.

At times, life offers all of us challenges seemingly impossible to get through. Navigating the seasons of life can be a guessing game. Each day can be a battle of endurance and will.

Even if you're currently experiencing a mountaintop, none of us can say we've always gotten it all right, all the time.

This life can be overwhelming *if we attempt it on our own.*

But consider these words of encouragement: This life is an amazing gift designed for abundance. God has more for us than what we have grown to settle for.

Wherever you're at right now, this book is about coming to grips with the reality that God has a plan – His Blueprint for life, as recorded in the Bible. In every page of Scripture, the great Architect declares how He designed life to be.

We all have much to learn about the Blueprint of God's Word that holds the key to life itself.

Let me share with you how God radically transformed who I am.

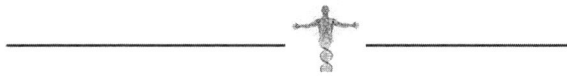

I Wept.

"What am I doing with my life? Is this all there is?"

I found myself asking these questions as I sat at my desk. Reality was finally setting in and I was nearing a breaking point. I never thought in a million years I would find myself in this place. I never thought I would experience this kind of heartache – certainly not under these self-inflicted circumstances. I was only twenty-five years old, but in that moment I truly believed my life had already seen its rise and fall. I felt lost and helpless. I was frantically searching for any sign of hope - any way out. Over and over I asked myself, "What happened? How did I get to this point? What have I done?" I kept asking these questions, trying to make sense of what went wrong.

The choices I made were now costing me dearly. Can you relate?

I'd been working in our family's business and things seemed wonderful. I thought I was doing pretty well. To those looking on, I'm sure everything looked like the American Dream. I'd been married to my wife Theresa for five years and we had two children. At first glance our relationship seemed good. It was far from perfect, but we painted a pretty picture when we needed to. I was making great money. I bought my dream car, a yellow Audi S4. It was beautiful. Every Sunday, we would get dressed up and do the "right" thing – take our family to church. On the surface everything looked good.

But things soon went from superficial to serious.

When my family's business took an unexpected downward turn, I found myself taking life by the horns and testing the waters of entrepreneurship. I had convinced myself that I could single-handedly tackle any adversity, and everything I needed would somehow fall into place. After all, this was my life and I was capable of shaping it the way I wanted.

It wasn't long before I accumulated thousands of dollars of debt. My Sunday-only relationship with God left me feeling hypocritical. My marriage was nothing more than a formality – two people living together with kids, having sex and paying bills. I had no real direction to stand on. Yet I never said a word about my problems to anyone. When people asked me how things were going, I smiled and said, "Everything's great!" But deep inside, I knew things weren't right. I knew my life was in trouble, but I kept pushing forward with my own stubborn strength, believing I was going to turn it around.

My failings led me into an addiction.

"I'm not an addict," I would tell myself. The guilt, secrecy, and shame of who I was becoming was real – and it began to haunt me every day. I struggled to look at myself in the mirror. I felt ashamed. I became engrossed in living vicariously through other people, seeking superficial highs to mask the reality of my inadequacies.

My newly formed business involved selling basketball apparel and putting on basketball events in the community, which put me in the spotlight. I received praise and notoriety from people, athletes, and even the local news. I fed off it and found it to be a great masking tool to cover up the pain and hurt I was feeling. The business itself had no future and was failing, but I just put on that smile and kept living life the way I wanted, believing that somehow I would turn it around.

Every area of my life was soon out of sync. I was empty. My home, marriage, career, finances, desire, passion, joy, peace, direction, hope – it was all empty.

So there I sat in a puddle of tears at a desk I couldn't pay for. I stared out across a retail space I owned with a lease I couldn't pay for. My eyes scanned over racks filled with inventory, and on the counter sat an empty cash register. It was 8:00 p.m. and cars were driving by one after another on the main highway in front of my store. Not one car was stopping to make a purchase – not even the tap of brake lights to signify that anyone had an interest to stop. Every set of headlights that passed was a reminder of how desperate I'd become. Each illuminated the errors of my ways.

The pretty picture I'd painted was being revealed for what it really was.

One by one, the cars passed and I watched the world go by.

I wept.

On my desk sat a picture of my wife Theresa – a reminder of how bad things were at home and how much I had let her and my children down. I had two young children who looked up to me, and yet, I spent so much time pursuing my own plans and priorities that I drifted apart from the very people I once held closest to my heart.

I never thought of myself as a guy who could ruin his life. "I'm Tim Cox Jr, I can figure this out!" I told myself, even as things spiraled out of control. I took a lot of stock in my ability to "MacGyver" life. I was determined to bring my plans to fruition.

Yet, in that moment, I wept.

I could do nothing on my own to correct the mistakes I had made. Maybe you've been there, maybe you're headed there, or maybe you just want to make sure you never get there. Whatever the case may be, I've been there. I had hit rock bottom. My hope was lost and my pride crushed. God was revealing to me my frailty.

Then God transformed my life with His unwavering truth.

I still remember it like it was yesterday. I humbled myself and began pouring my heart out to an Almighty God. I was hungry for something great and truly desperate for mercy. I raised both of my hands in the air and cried out, "God, I can't do it my way anymore. I don't want to. If you can put these pieces back together they're all yours. Here's my mess. I give you control. I'll follow your lead and walk the path you have for me – by Your design. Please help me!"

I can't really explain what happened next. An overwhelming peace came upon me. A weight was lifted off my shoulders. Although I knew I had a terrible mess to deal with, a sense of calmness reassured me that everything was going to be okay.

God used that desperate place to break me, teach me, and lead me into a new understanding of life. I learned that sometimes God allows us to become nothing so He can make us into everything He desires us to be.

My life changed forever that day, and I'm compelled to share with you what God has taught me since. It was the beginning of a complete overhaul of everything I thought I knew, as He introduced me to a whole new way of living.

Trust me when I say that I'm just an ordinary man loving an extraordinary God. He is worthy of all praise, glory, and honor.

The Blueprint

My story is not unique. Many Christians struggle with these kinds of questions:

- Why does life always have to be a struggle?
- If being a Christian is so great, why do I feel this way?
- What is my real purpose in life? Is this the life God intended?
- Why is my faith like a roller coaster? I'm not sure what I believe!

Ephesians 1:23 declares that the Church is "made full and complete by Christ." Is your faith full and complete? For years, my faith was nothing more than a façade. I read the Bible, but failed to become fully rooted in God's Word. I knew Jesus died for me, but I had never established the foundational building blocks of my faith. Without a firm foundation, my faith was built on sinking sand. I was still doing life by my own design.

Intellectual knowledge is one thing, but experiential understanding reveals something totally different.

Over the years, God led me through many different seasons of life. As of the writing of this book, I've been a pastor for six years. I planted a church in the poorest city of New York State and worked with hundreds of ordinary people who struggle with the challenges of everyday life. I've travelled different roads and experienced all sorts of ups and downs, as most of us do.

This book is not a feel good, overnight fix. I want to be real with you as I share what God has been faithful in teaching me from His Word. He breaks me, tests me, and leads me to places where I seemingly have no choice but to acknowledge His will for my life. He is faithful even as I stumble, always giving me a reassurance of His love, grace, and mercy. I am continually challenged to renew my mind and seek a whole new level of understanding. It's humbling, and not always easy.

At some point, we have to come to grips with the fact that God is in control. When the enemy convinces us that life is solely about following ourselves – pursuing our own desires and controlling our own destinies

– he removes the one true absolute that should anchor our souls, God's sovereignty over all things. The eternal truth of God's almighty design should captivate us in every way.

My heart and passion in writing this book is to help you firmly establish nine core building blocks of a faith that is full and complete. Each chapter focuses on God's Blueprint for a specific area of your life. As each chapter builds upon the next, I pray that you will gain knowledge of God's Word and actively apply it, gaining a true understanding to navigate through life the way God intends you to.

> *All Scripture is inspired by God and is useful to teach us what is true and to make us realize what is wrong in our lives. It corrects us when we are wrong and teaches us to do what is right.*
>
> *2 Timothy 3:16*

No matter where you've been, what you've done, or how little you know, you can experience lifechange. You don't have to purposely ready yourself for God. God readies you for His purpose. With God, your willingness matters more than your readiness. I wasn't prepared to start living by God's design, but by His grace He empowered me to accomplish more than I thought was possible (Ephesians 3:20). He can do the same for you.

Even in the midst of our failures, God showers us with His faithfulness and never-failing love. I pray that as you read this book, you'll find yourself hungry to learn, live, and experience the awesome peace found resting in the Creator's hand.

As we learn to live the Blueprint, we will experience the awesome riches of the Architect.

> *Follow my advice, my son; always treasure my commands. Obey my commands and live! Guard my instructions as you guard your own eyes. Tie them on your fingers as a reminder. Write them deep within your heart.*
>
> *Proverbs 7:1-3*

QUESTIONS. ADDITIONAL STUDY. APPLICATION.

Thoughts from the Introduction

We have a tendency to pretty what's not so pretty, bending the truth of situations so they don't seem as serious as they often are. We may bend the reality of our weight, career, relationships, or health, but in order to experience the true riches of the Architect, we must face the reality of our brokenness. If there is one area of your life where you need to be brutally honest, it's your relationship with God. This book is built on the awesome principle of God's Authority. The Bible is God's Blueprint for life. To experience a life that is full and complete, we must establish the core building blocks of the Architect's design.

Questions to Consider

If you were to describe your relationship with God in one sentence, what would it be?

What are your greatest struggles in life? Do you have a sense of direction to correct them?

On a scale of 1 to 10, how would you rank your understanding of God's Word?

Do you feel full and complete? Have you ever felt levels of fullness and/or completeness? If so, what was that like?

Do you think it is possible to experience a full and complete life outside of God's purpose and divine plan? Why?

Additional Verses to Study / How Can i Apply This?

- 1 Corinthians 2:13-16

- Proverbs 1:7

- Psalm 14:1-6

- Galatians 6:7-8

- 1 Peter 5:7

Building Blocks: Before i Move On...

☐ I'm hungry for God to do extraordinary things in my life.

☐ I can't ready myself for God's full purpose on my own, but I give Him all I am so He can ready me for everything He has in store.

☐ I'm prepared to open my heart so the truth of God's Word can take strong roots in my life (Proverbs 7:1-3).

☐ I'm committed to fully completing *The BLUEPRiNT: Living by the Architect's Design*.

Prayer

God, I know that I often try to take control and do life all on my own. I know You have a plan – a great design! Please help me to establish the building blocks of my faith so I can build my relationship with You on a firm foundation. Take my pieces and make a masterpiece. Amen.

CHAPTER 1
THE UNMOVED MOVER

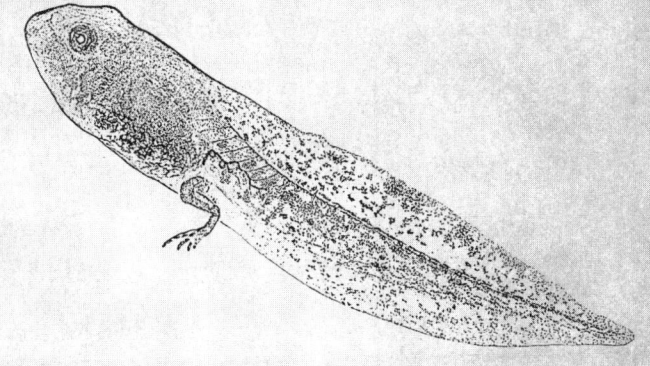

In the Beginning

In the beginning God created the heavens and the earth. The earth was formless and empty, and darkness covered the deep waters. And the Spirit of God was hovering over the surface of the waters.

Genesis 1:1-2

Every great work has a beginning and every great masterpiece has an artist. The Word of God is the true and authoritative recording of the beginning. We live in a world where things are rarely black and white. It seems that everything is open for interpretation and no one wants to offend anyone else's point of view. In today's world, we feel entitled to choose our own truths, carve out our own moral landscape, and define our own belief systems. Without any acknowledgement or consideration of a higher power, many simply live outside of true absolutes.

Over the years I've heard every argument and every angle. In the middle of all the noise, one thing remains constant and unwavering: This great design we call the universe has a designer. There is an Architect, and His Blueprint is recorded in His Word.

God has a specific design for your life. The only way to experience a full understanding of His design is to fully surrender to it. I know this may sound a little superficial or even cynical to some, but this is a powerful truth that God went to great lengths to deliver to us. God's Word was never meant to be watered-down, swept under the rug, or culturalized for easier consumption. It's is a perfect presentation of the Architect's plan. Word for word, page after page, God breathed insight on how all things are created and divinely orchestrated.

The Bible is more than a list of rules. It's more than a historical artifact. The Bible is more than a book. It's the very breath of God. That same breath of God that hovered over the dawn of Creation and spoke the universe into existence is now preserved for us to experience. The Bible is a living library of 66 books recorded by 40 writers over a period of 2,000 years. These writers were ordinary people like us, yet God used them to pen His Words. The Bible is without contradiction or fault. It's a perfect presentation of a perfect message. Prophets in the Old Testament who spoke of things to come were found to be flawlessly and meticulously accurate, not only in foretelling the events of the New Testament, but in the unrolling of all human history to the present day. The Bible stands alone with no other book of its kind in existence. The Truth that it contains has been changing lives for millennia.

For thousands of years men have studied, researched, and debated how the universe came into existence. We, as a society, have invested trillions of dollars into the exploration of space, time, and matter. Theories, ideas, and hypotheses are everywhere.

In the 13th century, the great theologian Thomas Aquinas expounded on five proofs of God's existence in his book *Summa Theologica* (Summary of Theology). Aquinas was captivated by the mere principle of motion and its evidence that there must be a grand Architect. You can break down his simple, yet direct approach to motion into four points.

- Some things are in motion
- An object not in motion cannot put itself in motion – it can only be moved by an outside force (a mover).
- An infinite chain of movers is impossible.
- Therefore, there must be an unmoved mover from whom all motion proceeds.

God is the Unmoved Mover. Though elementary in principle, Aquinas was making a very logical statement. If something moves, something had to move it. If something changes, something had to change it. All actions are caused by previous actions, but an infinite chain of cause-and-effect is impossible. At some point all cause-and-effect traces back to one origin. There had to be a beginning. Without a beginning point, nothing would exist.

Philosophers used to wonder if perhaps the universe is infinitely old. But this idea has been disproven. Today, there is a strong consensus among scientists that the universe had a beginning, because the universe is expanding. This expansion means that an infinitely old universe is impossible. Imagine "rewinding" the great tape of the universe and watching its expansion in reverse. You would see the universe get smaller and smaller, but it can't keep getting smaller forever. At some point, everything comes together. The universe did not always exist. There was a point in time when it came into existence. That point is the beginning.

It's the beginning that we often struggle with. Although it's now a universally accepted fact of science that the universe had a beginning, the great question still remains: what *caused* the universe to come into existence?

Without God, this question is impossible to answer. If nothing existed before the universe, and you can't get something from nothing, then how could anything exist at all?

The design of the universe requires a Designer. The Creation of the universe requires a Creator. Without an eternally existant Being to set the ball in motion, nothing would ever exist – not even time itself.

Some people struggle with accepting this awesome truth, but there is really no way around it. Maybe it's the fear of not wanting to recognize a Creator, or the uncertainty of our purpose in the wake of His power. But at the end of the day, no matter what the situation, no matter what the theory, no matter what is said, written, or taught, God still remains. He is the origin. He is the starting point. He is the Unmoved Mover from which everything else derives its existence. He is the same yesterday, today, and forever, and the Blueprint of His existence is on display for all to see.

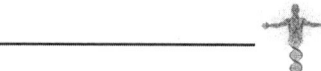

Day One

> *Then God said, "Let there be light," and there was light. And God saw that the light was good. Then he separated the light from the darkness. God called the light "day" and the darkness "night." And evening passed and morning came, marking the first day.*
>
> *Genesis 1:3-5*

Light.

Imagine what that must have been like! God spoke and from His mouth came light at 186,282 miles per second. In an instant, darkness had a direct opposite - a heavenly separation. This picture is so intense and so epic that it's hard for us to comprehend it.

How would you define "light?" How would you put it into words? How could you possibly describe light to a person born blind? Scientists cannot fully understand it. Even some of the greatest writers of our time struggle to describe it.

Light: "Something that makes vision possible."

-Merriam Webster's Dictionary

I have to chuckle when I read this. "Something." The benchmark for definition is stumped by "light." God's awesome power and creativity are far beyond what human language can express. Scientists have been studying light for centuries, and yet, to this day no one knows exactly what light is. There is still a great debate in science on whether light is a particle or a wave. It cannot be both, and yet, it has the characteristics of both. Light is a mystery that defies explanation.

The simple switch of a light bulb is a miracle. We may take credit for such inventions, but we are working with energy and matter already provided by God. Only God can create light from *nothing*. Imagine a world without light. And then suddenly, God speaks light into existence.

Don't we often take these things for granted? The concept of light has lost its luster. Can I challenge you to do something? Go into your closet and sit in the dark for a few minutes. Seriously. Sit there and imagine what it would be like to live in total darkness.

Are you sitting in the dark? (If you're reading this, you're not sitting in the dark)

Go sit there for a few minutes. Then reach out to the nearest light switch and embrace the power of light. Let it envelop you. Isn't it amazing what light does to darkness? What's in your closet? What color are the walls? What needs to be cleaned? What about that spider web? What hidden treasures did you find?

Light changes everything!

Day Two

Then God said, "Let there be a space between the waters, to separate the waters of the heavens from the waters of the earth." And that is what happened. God made this space to separate the waters of the earth from the waters of the heavens. God called the space "sky." And evening passed and morning came, marking the second day.

Genesis 1:6-8

God created a firmament – our atmosphere. It divides the waters below (the oceans) from the waters above (water vapor in the form of clouds). Most people, including myself, have no real clue how wonderful the design of our atmosphere is. Without our atmosphere's specific elements and structure, we wouldn't be able to survive. It's an awesome pavilion given to us by the grand Architect to shield us, protect us, and keep us. It's a supernatural bubble enabling us to experience life while being suspended in the middle of a universe that declares His majesty.

Our atmosphere is the air that we experience everyday. It consists of 78% nitrogen, 21% oxygen, 1% water vapor, and a miniscule amount of other gases like argon and carbon dioxide. This is the perfect formula for life. What would the world be like with no atmosphere? Life would suffocate. Imagine a world with an atmosphere made of toxic gases. Life would be poisoned. Of all the planets that have been discovered, only Earth has an atmosphere with the right balance of elements to support life. As animals breathe oxygen and exhale carbon dioxide, plants absorb carbon dioxide and produce oxygen. It's a symbiotic relationship only God could have orchestrated.

But our atmosphere does more than just give us air to breathe. It also contains an ozone layer that shields us from the sun's dangerous ultraviolet radiation. It acts as a greenhouse, keeping the earth at the proper temperature. It recycles our water as ocean water evaporates to form clouds, clouds give rain to plants all over the world, and rainwater flows back to the oceans. It's a perfect cycle that has been going on every day for ages.

Perhaps the most amazing thing about our atmosphere – and the thing we most easily take for granted – is that it allows sound to exist. A sound wave is simply a vibration of particles. There is no sound in the vacuum of outer space because space is empty – there are no particles to transmit the vibration. Air molecules in our atmosphere provide the perfect medium for transmitting sound. When you clap your hands, you're creating a vibration in the air – particles bumping into other particles, which bump into other particles, and so on until they bump into your eardrum, causing an electrical signal to go to your brain.

It all happens instantly, and we easily take it for granted. But without air molecules to transmit the vibrations we call "sound," hearing would be impossible.

Without our atmosphere, we would not be able to breathe, drink water, or hear music. The earth would be nothing but deadly silence.

When God spoke the firmament into existence, He laid the foundation for life by His perfect design.

It's amazing to see God's awesome creativity in things like the water cycle and the oxygen cycle.

Imagine a barren, desert world with no air, no sound, no clouds, and no life.

If you lived on that world, and it was the only place you ever knew, would you have the creativity to imagine something as glorious and magnificent as vast oceans, thunderstorms, living creatures, or music?

Would you expect all these things to just happen without the Blueprint of an ingenious Architect?

I wouldn't be able to imagine these things, much less create them *from scratch!*

But that's exactly what God did.

Day Three

Then God said, "Let the waters beneath the sky flow together into one place, so dry ground may appear." And that is what happened. God called the dry ground "land" and the waters "seas." And God saw that it was good. Then God said, "Let the land sprout with vegetation— every sort of seed-bearing plant, and trees that grow seed-bearing fruit. These seeds will then produce the kinds of plants and trees from which they came." And that is what happened. The land produced vegetation—all sorts of seed-bearing plants, and trees with seed-bearing fruit. Their seeds produced plants and trees of the same kind. And God saw that it was good. And evening passed and morning came, marking the third day.

Genesis 1:9-13

This place we call home is truly remarkable. From the deserts of Mongolia to the waters of the Caspian Sea, from the high peaks of the Rocky Mountains to the great valleys of the Blyde River Canyon, the landscape of the earth is a work of creative genius. The fact that we can enjoy everyday life on this awesome planet is a miracle in itself. The dynamics and engineering of our world are beyond understanding.

Did you know that the earth rotates on its axis at 1,000 miles per hour? At the same time, the earth also travels around the sun at 66,700 miles per hour. Meanwhile, the sun and everything orbiting it are moving around the center of the Milky Way galaxy at 559,234 miles per hour. And just when you thought things couldn't possibly be moving any faster, astronomers have discovered that our entire galaxy is on the move at 2,235,600 miles per hour.

Right now, as you read this very page, you are traveling through space on a spinning ball of rock that is moving around a sun that is moving around the center of a galaxy that is itself moving! At any given moment, your body is traveling at millions of miles per hour. And yet, your coffee isn't even spilling. That is hard to fathom. Just thinking about it makes me feel like I'm having a post roller coaster moment.

We don't realize the motion because everything is moving together – your coffee cup is moving at the same speed you are, so from your perspective, it appears to be standing still. And even though the earth is spinning extremely fast, we don't fly off of it because the earth's gravity is perfectly proportioned to hold us in place. Too little gravity, and there would be no atmosphere. Too much, and we wouldn't be able to move. Our planet is perfectly designed – Blueprinted – for life.

The center of the earth is made up of an inner core and an outer core. The inner core is solid iron and nickel, the perfect material to handle immense pressure. It weighs 30,000,000,000,000,000,000 pounds and yet it's suspended by liquid metal in the outer core. Like a raging river, the molten liquid of the outer core moves intensely around the inner core, creating a magnetic field. This magnetic field shields us from deadly radiation from the sun, that would otherwise kill all life on earth in an instant.

What about vegetation? Did you ever stop and think about pollination or germination? Think about those processes – incredible detail and flawless synchronization. Season after season, insect after insect, seed after seed, weather, sunlight, wind power, hydration, and continual, never-ending processes sustain life year after year.

Have you ever marveled at how a tiny acorn can grow into a giant oak tree? A seed can lay dormant for hundreds of years, and yet, as soon as it's planted and watered, it begins to grow. Israeli scientists discovered a 2,000 year-old date palm seed while excavating ruins at Mount Masada. When planted, this ancient seed grew and produced fresh, sweet, edible dates! God gave seeds incredible longevity!

Trees are an awesome revelation of God's genius. Not only do trees provide us with oxygen to breathe and fruit to eat, but they also give us shade on a hot day, provide habitats for millions of species, filter and purify the air, and hold soil in place, preventing erosion that would make agriculture impossible. If God hadn't given us the gift of trees, we wouldn't be here!

Have you ever wondered how a tree is able to transport water from its roots all the way up to its leaves, branches, and buds? Inside a tree, the water literally flows uphill! This is because of an awesome principle of physics God created called capillary action. When water is compressed into a narrow tube such as a tree's internal veins, the adhesion force between the liquid and the wall of the tube is more powerful than the force of gravity, allowing the liquid to flow uphill.

Grab a paper towel and dip the end of it in water, and you'll see this process in action. The water will gradually climb up the towel until gravity slows it to a stop.

From the vastness of the universe to the trunk of a single tree, God's design is on display.

Day Four

Then God said, "Let lights appear in the sky to separate the day from the night. Let them be signs to mark the seasons, days, and years. Let these lights in the sky shine down on the earth." And that is what happened. God made two great lights—the larger one to govern the day, and the smaller one to govern the night. He also made the stars. God set these lights in the sky to light the earth, to govern the day and night, and to separate the light from the darkness. And God saw that it was good. And evening passed and morning came, marking the fourth day.

Genesis 1:14-19

I could write for hours on the vastness of our universe or even our own solar system. Through the process of nuclear fusion, the core of the sun burns at an amazing 27,000,000 degrees Fahrenheit. By articulate design, our earth is located 93,000,000 miles from the sun and it takes eight minutes for the sun's energy to reach us. By the time it arrives, enough energy has been lost to provide the perfect temperature for sustainable life. 27,000,000 degrees Fahrenheit, and yet all you feel is the warmth of a 75 degree summer breeze on your face – energy that was sent eight minutes ago from 93,000,000 miles away.

Did you know that you could fit 1,000,000 earths inside the sun? What's even more amazing is that the sun is a relatively small star compared to the billions of other stars in space.

Take a look, for example, at Betelgeuse, a red giant star. Betelgeuse is large enough to hold a billion of our suns, and it's 14,000 times brighter.

Let me put it to you this way. Go outside and hop in your car. Start driving to Betelgeuse, which happens to be 600 light-years away. Driving at 65 miles per hour, it would take you over six billion years to get there. When you arrive, start driving around the equator of this massive star. At 65 miles per hour, it would take you over 5,000 years to drive one time around the star. This is close to impossible to fathom – but we haven't even scratched the surface.

Before the telescope was invented, it was thought that the 1000-2000 stars visible to the naked eye were all the stars that existed. Now that we have the technology to search the sky with telescopes, we realize just how wrong we were.

There are actually *billions* of stars in our galaxy. Not only that, but many of the lights in the sky that we thought were stars are actually entire galaxies. There are billions of galaxies in space, each containing billions of stars. *Billions of billions.* The vastness of Creation is beyond comprehension.

Feeling small yet?

There are more jaw-dropping wonders in the sky than just stars. The largest diamond on earth is called the "Winston Legacy." It weighs 101 carats, and sold for $26,700,000 at auction. But in 2004, astronomers discovered something far more impressive – so impressive that the Winston Legacy looks like a child's toy in comparison.

The largest diamond ever discovered floats in space fifty light-years away, and weighs 10,000,000,000,000,000,000,000,000,000,000,000 carats.

It was forged in the heart of a massive star that has since burned out, leaving behind a jewel of indescribable value.

I don't know about you, but I find this incredibly humbling. All of our wealth and all of our knowledge is absolutely nothing when placed before Almighty God. We are completely incapable of even beginning to imagine the riches of His wealth, power, and wisdom. Psalm 19:1 says:

> *The heavens declare the glory of God; and the firmament shows His handiwork.*

This passage reminds me of when my oldest son, Kobe, was about six years old. We were out getting some groceries and it was late. When we arrived home it was dark and I waited for him to get out of the car so I could guide him to the house. It was one of those nights when the sky was clear and stars looked twice the size they normally do. Like thousands of diamonds on a dark canvas, the night sky danced in illumination. It was truly a wonderful sight.

After taking several steps with his head tilted back, gazing into the heavens, Kobe stopped and stared. After a few moments he said, "Wow! Isn't God amazing?" Even through the eyes of a child it's easy to see that God's handiwork is far too vast for human explanation.

Day Five

> *Then God said, "Let the waters swarm with fish and other life. Let the skies be filled with birds of every kind." So God created great sea creatures and every living thing that scurries and swarms in the water, and every sort of bird—each producing offspring of the same kind. And God saw that it was good. Then God blessed them, saying, "Be fruitful and multiply. Let the fish fill the seas, and let the birds multiply on the earth." And evening passed and morning came, marking the fifth day.*
>
> *Genesis 1:20-23*

God said, "with an abundance" on day five.

Every spring on opening day of bass season, my family and I go to my parent's camp located on the Sacandaga River, nestled in the Adirondack Mountains of upstate New York. I enjoy fishing the river because the fish are strong from fighting the current. When you hook a fish, there's a whole series of adrenalin-pumping questions that race through your mind. What kind of fish is it? How big is the fish? Is it a "keeper"?

Then, all of a sudden, the fish breaks the surface, revealing itself. The sight of a bass jumping out of the water, shaking and rolling, is a pretty exciting sight to behold. As great as those moments are, a bass is just one of an abundance of aquatic creatures that God created. Dolphins, tuna, shrimp, carp, blowfish, octopi, seahorses, lobster, clownfish, stingrays, jellyfish – just think about the diversity of our underwater ecosystems. From microorganisms to the enormous whale shark – which can grow up to 60 feet long and weigh up to 15 tons - God's Creation is unmatched.

What about frogs? Have you ever stopped and thought about what it must be like for a frog in its younger years? Tough days of puberty, for sure. One day you're swimming around as a tadpole and the next thing you know, you start sprouting legs! Talk about awkward moments. How do you explain that to your friends when you're just chilling in the shallows of the eastside?

The creatures of the sky are no less gripping. The beauty of the pelican, the great wings of the eagle, the intricacies of the hummingbird – all the fowl of the air were designed with meticulous detail and awesome beauty. Flamingos sleep on one leg. The white-throated needletail can fly at speeds near 105 miles per hour. The owl can see in the dark. The peregrine falcon can spot a pigeon five miles away. Some species of parrots have been known to fly over 500 miles a day to find a source of food.

Millennia before man figured out flight, God said, "let birds fly," and they flew. On December 17, 1903, after years of trial and error, Orville and Wilbur Wright left the surface of the earth and took flight on the world's first airplane. But the principles of flight today – after all these years of research and development – are still the same as they were when God spoke the word "fly" so many ages ago.

Day Six

Then God said, "Let the earth produce every sort of animal, each producing offspring of the same kind—livestock, small animals that scurry along the ground, and wild animals." And that is what happened. God made all sorts of wild animals, livestock, and small animals, each able to produce offspring of the same kind. And God saw that it was good.

Then God said, "Let us make human beings in our image, to be like us. They will reign over the fish in the sea, the birds in the sky, the livestock, all the wild animals on the earth, and the small animals that scurry along the ground."

So God created human beings in his own image. In the image of God he created them; male and female he created them. Then God blessed them and said, "Be fruitful and multiply. Fill the earth and govern it. Reign over the fish in the sea, the birds in the sky, and all the animals that scurry along the ground."

Then God said, "Look! I have given you every seed-bearing plant throughout the earth and all the fruit trees for your food. And I have given every green plant as food for all the wild animals, the birds in the sky, and the small animals that scurry along the ground—everything that has life." And that is what happened. Then God looked over all he had made, and he saw that it was very good! And evening passed and morning came, marking the sixth day.

Genesis 1:24-31

I certainly don't want to take anything away from the magnificence of the insect, reptile, and animal kingdoms. A couple years ago I had the opportunity to visit the Cincinnati Zoo with my family. As we walked around, it didn't take long to become overwhelmed with the wide array of amazing creatures. I can remember looking across a short ravine at white tigers. As the sun glistened off their striped coats, their sheer presence was overwhelming and intimidating.

Think about some of the great creatures you've seen or studied. Consider the vast differences between them. The powerful tail of the Brachiosaurus. The great speed of the cheetah. The long neck of the giraffe. The striking power of the cobra. The camouflaging magic of chameleon. The strength of the black bear. The work ethic of the honey bee.

God's Creation is immense in scope and diversity!

Did you know that the housefly always hums in the key of F? Fleas can jump up to 200 hundred times their height. Elephants can smell water up to three miles away. The beaver's teeth never stop growing. Bats always turn left when leaving a cave – the true mascot of NASCAR. The arctic ground squirrel literally freezes solid every winter – its body temperature dropping to 26 degrees Fahrenheit and its heart beating less than once a minute – and yet, when it thaws out in the spring, it's still as alive and healthy as ever!

God gave man dominion over the land to live off of it and multiply. I find it inspiring that God created animals that would produce nourishment and care for humanity. Chickens lay eggs, cows produce dairy, and sheep grow wool. Every detail of the Architect's plan is exact and purposeful.

Simply put, our world is a canvas on which the great Architect painted life according to His Blueprint. Whether it's the billions of stars that light up the night sky, the breath of fresh air you take in every morning, the glass of milk you enjoy before bed, or the crickets that play sweet music as you fall asleep, God has declared His authority!

Yet amazingly, the declaration of God as the great Architect is often opposed in today's world. What do you believe? Do you see the grand design of the universe, or is everything around you a coincidence? I believe that if we simply open our eyes to the evidence before us, we'll see beyond the shadow of a doubt that God is real.

The very same God who breathed the stars into existence is the one who designed and created you. He loves you. He desires to lead you. He is for you. Although we may try to figure this life out on our own, aspiring to achieve our own goals and dreams, God is in control.

God's Word declares direction for your purpose, provision, and peace. Each and every day we make decisions and choices, actively shaping our lives. We are all moving. The question is what – or who – is moving you? Are you moved by the worries and fears of this life? Or are you moved by the Unmoved Mover?

The great Blueprint awaits.

> *In the beginning, Lord, you laid the foundation of the earth and made the heavens with your hands.*
>
> *Hebrews 1:10*

QUESTIONS. ADDITIONAL STUDY. APPLICATION.

Thoughts from Chapter 1: The Unmoved Mover

The building block of Creation is a critical first step in anchoring your faith. You can't claim the promises of the New Testament without your faith being anchored in the truths declared in Genesis. Many find themselves on the wrong side of the coin when it comes to Creation. You don't have to prove what has already been proven. The world tries to prove that God is not who His handiwork says He is, but the heavens declare the majesty of God. Be bold in your understanding of who put all things into motion. Rest in knowing that days one through six were just for you. He created everything you see and experience, just to show you how much He loves you. He is in control!

Questions to Consider

Have you fully come to grips with the fact that God is the Creator of the universe?

Are there any areas of Creation that you struggle with?

Do you find yourself trying to defend or prove to others that God is the Creator? If so, how often do you leave feeling defeated or doubtful? Why?

What is your favorite part of God's handiwork? How often do you bask in the incredible magnitude of His Creation?

Is the Unmoved Mover moving you each day? How does the magnitude of His creativity, detail, and design convict you when it comes to the areas of your life you often want full control over?

Additional Verses to Study / How Can i Apply This?

- Romans 1:19-20

- Hebrews 11:1-3

- Hebrews 1:10-12

- Isaiah 40:12-31

- Job 38-39

Building Blocks: Before i Move On…

☐ I have a knowledge and understanding of each day of Creation.

☐ I believe that God is the Architect who not only spoke all things into existence, but also has laid out the Blueprint for my life.

☐ I'm committed to resting in the reality of Creation. I won't allow myself to fall into the trap of trying to prove what is already proven, but rather declare what is absolute – God is the Author of Creation.

☐ I desire to live a life that is moved by the Unmoved Mover.

Prayer

God, I pray that You captivate my heart with the awesomeness of Your Creation. Help me to take the time to experience the power of Your declaration that's on display before my very eyes. Convict my heart with the reality of Your AUTHORity. I give you my life so you can move me in the direction you have for me. As I continue to learn Your Word, please guide each area of my life to accomplish a full and complete work. Amen.

CHAPTER 2

THE BREATH AND THE BARRIER

Then the LORD God formed the man from the dust of the ground. He breathed the breath of life into the man's nostrils, and the man became a living person.

Genesis 2:7

The God of the universe – the Creator of all things – bent down and formed man from the dust of the ground. As endless and dynamic as our universe is, the human body is just as staggering. In Genesis 1:26, God says:

"...Let us make human beings in our image..."

We were created in God's image. God created us with feelings and emotions. We were born with a natural desire to love and be loved. At our very core, we are all people of unique structure, style, and expression.

The human body's skeletal structure consists of 206 bones, each one serving a specific purpose. These bones work in conjunction with over 650 muscles. Each muscle is assisted by layers of muscle tissue. Some of our muscles are voluntary – directly attached to our central nervous system. Other muscles are involuntary and work on their own (swallowing, goose-bumps, blinking, breathing, and the heart beating). The central nervous system is directly connected to the brain, allowing us to send signals to various muscles and instantly create movement.

Look at your finger. Now tell it to move back and forth. Now tell it to stop. Amazing. In a split second your brain processes a command and then sends an electrical signal through a specific channel of neurons that communicate with one another through a series of instantaneous chemical reactions. There are over 100,000,000 neurons in your body and yet your brain is able to determine an exact course of communication to create muscular movement instantly.

Our bodies have over 100,000,000,000,000 cells. If you were to put them end-to-end you would have enough to circle the earth four and a half times. In every cell you find DNA specific to you. Your DNA is your unique genetic code, determined at the moment of your conception. This code determines your physical characteristics and your cells read this code to know what your eyes, skin, hair, and other features should look like.

If you were to stretch out a single set of DNA from a single cell, it would be about six and half feet long. Imagine taking a rope six and a half feet long and neatly wrapping it up until it could fit inside a cell too small to be seen without a microscope. It seems like an impossible task, and yet, that's exactly what God did when He created DNA.

That six and half foot strand is just one set of DNA from one of the 100,000,000,000,000 cells in your body. If you took all the DNA strands in your body and laid them end-to-end, you'd have a strand long enough to go to the moon and back 6,000 times. That's how much personal data is stored inside your body to make you the unique individual you are.

Creating just one human being would be amazing enough, but God went a step further and gave humans the ability to reproduce. The process of reproduction is literally miraculous. Think about the amazing process of a baby's 40-week development in the womb. Imagine the trillions of cells forming arms and legs, fingers and toes, a functioning brain that defies scientific explanation, eyesight through the pairing of 1,000,000 optical nerve endings, a sense of taste, and a sense of smell. The time comes, and after hours of labor contractions, a miracle enters the world. It is in this moment we are reminded of Genesis 2:7,

> "...He breathed the breath of life into the man's nostrils..."

When Theresa and I were expecting our third child we thought we were old pros. We had already been through the labor process before and things had been smooth overall with very little concern. The day came and it was time for Josie's arrival. After about twelve hours of labor the time came for the delivery. I waited with great anticipation.

Theresa struggled and struggled, and in my gut I knew something wasn't right – this wasn't like the other times. Finally, after what seemed like an eternity of intense pushing, Josie's head appeared. However, the umbilical chord was wrapped around her neck. The doctor quickly unwrapped the chord and pulled her free. An alarming and a terrible feeling gripped the pit of my stomach as I looked on. Josie was blue in color and unresponsive.

I remember Theresa crying and asking the doctor what was wrong. He responded calmly, "She's just stunned." I didn't know what that meant, but for me the world was standing still. I watched as the doctor took Josie's motionless body over to a table and began to roll her over and over. It looked like he was making pizza dough. Every second that passed felt like a thousand years. All of a sudden, she gasped and whimpered with a first breath.

Breathing never sounded so good.

Imagine what it was like for Adam. God formed him from the dust of the earth and in one defining moment breathed into him the breath of life. That same breath that breathed the stars penetrated Adam's lungs, and he became a living soul. This breath of God is more than just air. The Spirit of God breathed eternal life into Adam's spirit. The moment Adam's lifeless body experienced the breath of God, Adam came alive – physically and spiritually. God is the Author of life and we were designed to experience His breath.

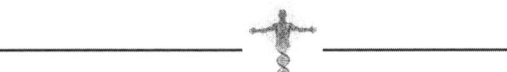

Garden Walks

Then the LORD God took the man and put him in the garden of Eden to tend and keep it.

Genesis 2:15

Reading through Genesis 1-2, you'll find that God desired great things for Adam. God spent five out of the six days of Creation building a universe with the anticipation of mankind. Once God formed Adam and gave him life, God immediately began to establish a relationship with him. God placed Adam in a perfect, lush environment with vegetation, animals, and fresh water. God realized that Adam was alone and in need of a companion, so God gave him a wife.

Everything was perfect. There was no sorrow, no pain, no suffering, no regret, no pressure, no worries. Adam and Eve had a daily relationship with their Creator. God was personal with them. God communicated with them. He spent time with them and established a powerful and compassionate interaction with them. God's love is overwhelmingly evident in Genesis 1-2.

God gave man dominion over everything He created. Adam spent his early days naming animals as God presented them before him. "Name this one, Adam!" 'What do you think about this one?" "I knew you'd really like this one!" God was for Adam. God desired to bless him and provide for him.

The Barrier

But the LORD God warned him, "You may freely eat the fruit of every tree in the garden—except the tree of the knowledge of good and evil. If you eat its fruit, you are sure to die."

The serpent was the shrewdest of all the wild animals the LORD God had made. One day he asked the woman, "Did God really say you must not eat the fruit from any of the trees in the garden?"

"Of course we may eat fruit from the trees in the garden," the woman replied. "It's only the fruit from the tree in the middle of the garden that we are not allowed to eat. God said, 'You must not eat it or even touch it; if you do, you will die.'"

"You won't die!" the serpent replied to the woman. "God knows that your eyes will be opened as soon as you eat it, and you will be like God, knowing both good and evil."

The woman was convinced. She saw that the tree was beautiful and its fruit looked delicious, and she wanted the wisdom it would give her. So she took some of the

> *fruit and ate it. Then she gave some to her husband, who was with her, and he ate it, too.*
>
> *Then the LORD God asked the woman, "What have you done?" "The serpent deceived me," she replied. "That's why I ate it."*
>
> *Genesis 2:16-17, 3:1-6, 3:13*

Recently, I was leading a Bible study and we were discussing the Garden of Eden. Adam and Eve had a beautiful invitation to fellowship with God in a perfect environment. There was no fighting, peer pressure, stress, or anxiety. They didn't have to deal with a culture that was going in an ungodly direction. Adam and Eve were experiencing exactly what God designed.

After an hour of discussing this, our Bible study group fell silent. We sat for a few moments, each person unwilling to leave that place. We all knew what happened next.

God gave Adam and Eve free will. Like us, they had the ability to make decisions. God designed their relationship with Him to be one of willingness and desire. God could have created Adam and Eve to be robots, serving Him faithfully without any choice in the matter. But relationship requires decision. God gave us free will because He wants a relationship with us. He wants children who decide to honor Him, love Him, and walk with Him – not because they have no choice, but because they *want* to.

There was just one simple rule – one tree that Adam and Eve could not eat from. Adam and Eve had the entire Garden – the entire universe – at their fingertips. They had peace in their hearts, joy in their spirits, and the fullness of a daily connection with their Creator. They were complete. They knew no wrong and no guilt.

> *This great dragon—the ancient serpent called the devil, or Satan, the one deceiving the whole world—was thrown down to the earth with all his angels.*
>
> *Revelation 12:9*

The enemy of God is the opposite of everything God is. God is life. The devil is death. Satan despises God's power and holiness. Equally disturbing is his hatred for God's Creation. From the beginning, Satan has waged a shrewd and deceitful war on everything God created. God loves us while the enemy seeks to destroy us.

Satan – under the guise of a snake – was precise in his persuasion of Eve. He didn't discuss the pros and cons. He had no concern for Eve's wellbeing. He dominated the conversation as though there was very little at stake and the world to be gained. He directly opposed God's Word in a convincing ploy. The devil was fully aware that if Adam and Eve were to experience the knowledge of both good and evil, he would have the opportunity to destroy the Blueprint God had established.

As a pastor, one of the most frequent questions I'm asked is, "If God knew we were going to sin and rebel against Him, why did He create us?"

It's a good question. I believe the answer reveals the Father's love for us.

One day my oldest daughter, Hailey, asked me this same question. She was seven years old at the time. After some thought, I responded, "Do you think Daddy loves you?"

She answered, "Yes!"

I asked, "Do you think that Daddy wants the absolute best for you?"

"Yes!"

Then I asked a tougher question: "Do you always do what I ask you to do?"

Reluctantly, she said, "No."

I responded, "Do you sometimes get hurt or get in trouble when you disobey?"

"Yes, it's usually not good," she said.

I said, "You're right. I love you and I want the absolute best for you. I would do anything for you. I would even die for you if I had to. But Mommy and Daddy knew before we even had you that you would sometimes disobey. We knew you would sometimes get hurt, and we knew you would sometimes hurt us. We knew that raising you wouldn't always be easy. There would sometimes be challenges, struggles, and heartache. But we also knew that in the end, the love we share would make it all worth it. We knew the joy that comes from our relationship would far outweigh the pain that comes from it."

A smile came over her face, as if to say, "I get it!"

When Adam and Eve disobeyed God, His heart broke. God watched. He grieved. God wanted to intervene, but His desire for a real relationship with them held Him back. With one simple act of disobedience, Adam and Eve's eyes opened to evil.

God took Adam and Eve from the Garden of Eden. From that day forward, they lived in a sinful world. Yet God never forsook them. He still desired to have an eternal relationship with them.

As Adam and Eve had children and the human population increased, sin was passed on to all people. Romans 5:12 declares:

> When Adam sinned, sin entered the world. Adam's sin brought death, so death spread to everyone, for everyone sinned.

The sad reality is that you and I are born with a sinful nature. We are born imperfect people. We are born incomplete – with an empty void inside of us that can only be filled by God. We need Him. He wants us.

Sin separated us. But love brought us a Savior.

The Seed of Salvation

For the first time, Adam and Eve were ashamed to be in the presence of God. Yet God called out to them. And immediately, He promised redemption.

> *Then the LORD God said to the serpent, "Because you have done this, you are cursed more than all animals, domestic and wild. You will crawl on your belly, groveling in the dust as long as you live. And I will cause hostility between you and the woman, and between your offspring and her offspring. He will strike your head, and you will strike his heel."*
>
> *Genesis 3:14-15*

God wages war against evil and promises imminent victory. The very Creation that became separated from God through sinful disobedience would one day bring a Savior to destroy sin forever. God declared that Satan would be crushed under the feet of the Savior, but ultimately it would cost the Savior His life.

In the years that followed, great prophets predicted the coming of the Savior. There were over 360 prophecies made over a span of 4,000 years. There is one Savior, one King of Kings, one Messiah, who fulfilled these prophecies to the last detail.

His name is Jesus.

Mathematics professors Peter W. Stoner and Dr. Robert C. Newman calculated the probability of a person fulfilling just 48 of the prophecies of the Old Testament as being 1 in 10,000,000,000,000,000,000,000, 000,000,000,000,000,000,000,000,000,000,000,000,000,000,000, 000,000,000,000,000,000,000,000,000,000,000,000,000,000,000, 000,000,000,000,000,000,000,000,000,000.

That's 157 zeros.

God loves us so much that He sent his only Son to lay down His life for our sins. Jesus left the splendor of Heaven to be born of a virgin in a filthy manger. He dwelt among us. He was tempted and tried just as we are and yet He never sinned. His words changed our world forever and His power touched the lives of many. He trained disciples, calling ordinary people to accomplish extraordinary things. He spoke boldly and denounced the vain religiosity of the day. He was a friend of sinners and purposefully sought out those who were rejected and in need.

Jesus was countercultural. He came not to praise the "righteous" but to love sinners and bring them to repentance. He didn't engross Himself in the self-glorifying rituals of the religious elite, but humbled Himself to serve the poorest and most detested individuals – even tax collectors and prostitutes. His message was undeniably loud and clear.

> *Jesus replied, "'You must love the Lord your God with all your heart, all your soul, and all your mind.' This is the first and greatest commandment. A second is equally important: 'Love your neighbor as yourself.'"*
>
> *Matthew 22:37-39*

Jesus' teachings are a Blueprint for our lives. He provides precise plans that include our redemption, hope, joy, and peace.

He lays the foundation for a healthy home and delivers insight into financial stewardship and success.

He provides specific instructions for handling temptations, trials, persecution, relationship struggles, unforgiveness, and bitterness.

He orchestrates the very Rock on which the Church is founded and commissions us to spread the glory of God to every nation.

In three years of ministry on the earth, Jesus Christ changed the world.

Salvation

> *For God made Christ, who never sinned, to be the offering for our sin, so that we could be made right with God through Christ.*
>
> *2 Corinthians 5:21*

Jesus was hated by many. Religious leaders were determined to eradicate His teachings. He was wrongly accused and placed on trial for crimes He never committed. The people hated Him so much that they voted to release a mass murderer on death row and have Jesus executed instead.

Imagine the love it must have taken to endure that kind of rejection from the very ones you came to save.

He was taken to a courtyard and beaten beyond recognition. Drops of blood fell from His body. Soldiers spit on Him and made a mockery of His rightful place as King of Kings. They took a crown of thorns and pressed it deep into His skull, each thorn embedding itself as blood poured down His brow.

They took Him and placed a Cross on His back and demanded that He carry it. With His back cut open, His beard ripped out, and His head crowned with thorns, Jesus took the Cross and began to make His journey to Golgotha – the "Place of the Skull." Weak and unable to go on, Jesus fell, each time trying to regain the strength to carry the Cross we were meant to bear.

Finally, He arrived on top of Mt. Calvary beaten, broken, and bleeding. Soldiers tore off His clothes, laid Him across the wooden beams of the Cross, and hammered nails into His hands and feet.

In that moment, Jesus thought of you. His love for you held Him to the Cross as they raised it up and drove it into the ground, suspending the Savior of the world between Heaven and earth.

Jesus Christ took your sins, my sins, and the sins of the whole world – past, present, and future – upon Himself. He never sinned, yet He took all of our faults and failures. He took the punishment we deserve upon Himself. He could have called Heaven's armies to rescue Him, and yet, despite all of His anguish, He endured – because of love.

The sins of the world were so dark that God the Father was forced to turn and look the other way as Jesus cried out, "Why have you abandoned me?" (Matthew 27:46, Mark 15:34).

The very pain that you're struggling with right now – your despair, your hopelessness, your uncertainty – Jesus was there.

Soldiers jammed a spear into His side and blood pooled up around the foot of the Cross. Isaiah 53:5 tells us that "he was pierced for our rebellion, crushed for our sins. He was beaten so we could be whole. He was whipped so we could be healed."

In a moment that changed the course of history forever, Jesus Christ experienced your death. He called out with one last breath and said, "It is finished!" (John 19:30). He experienced your separation from God.

He paid the price.

His disciples took His body and buried Him in a tomb. A stone was placed over the entrance, sealing the Savior's death.

I am so thankful the story doesn't end here.

On the third day, Jesus rose from the dead. The same Spirit of God that breathed life into Adam in the beginning also breathed the breath of life into the Savior of the world, and He arose from the grave victorious.

Nothing could hold Him down. He conquered death and made a way for us to experience victory over it. Sin had separated us from God, but Jesus bridged that gap when He took our sins to the grave and left them there.

This is the greatest story ever told. Salvation is the greatest gift ever offered.

No matter who you are, and no matter what your past has been, Salvation is available for you today. When Jesus rose from the grave on the third day, He gave you the opportunity to be forgiven and experience a relationship with God.

One Way, One Blueprint

Jesus told him, "I am the way, the truth, and the life. No one can come to the Father except through me."

John 14:6

There is only one plan of Salvation. The great Architect has one Blueprint for life and it starts at the foot of the Cross. Jesus is the only way for us to experience a relationship with the Father.

Over the years, Satan has proposed many false religions and philosophies that have obscured the plan of redemption. But there still remains only one way, and His name is Jesus Christ.

I've had countless people tell me that they believe in God, and that they are "good" people. But no matter how hard we try, no matter how "good" we are, we are still born with sin, separated from God, and in desperate need of redemption. Scripture tells us that our greatest feats of righteousness are as dirty rags to a Holy God. Romans 3:10 declares:

> *As the Scriptures say, "No one is righteous—not even one."*

Eternal life in God's presence is a gift so infinitely valuable that we would need to be perfectly righteous to deserve it. But the reality is, we are all imperfect people. No matter how "good" we are by the world's standards, we fall short of God's infinite perfection.

Our "good" is not good enough. We are incapable of saving ourselves. Jesus had to step in and make Salvation possible for us.

Ephesians 2:8-9 declares:

> *"God saved you by his grace when you believed. And you can't take credit for this; it is a gift from God. Salvation is not a reward for the good things we have done, so none of us can boast about it."*

Salvation is a free gift from God made possible by the sacrifice of Jesus Christ. All we need to do is accept the gift by placing our faith in Him.

Romans 10:9-10 clearly lays out the Blueprint for Salvation:

> *If you confess with your mouth that Jesus is Lord and believe in your heart that God raised him from the dead, you will be saved. For it is by believing in your heart that you are made right with God, and it is by confessing with your mouth that you are saved.*

Your Salvation is secured by the sacrificial love of the Father and sealed by the eternal power of the Holy Spirit – the very breath of God that raised Jesus Christ from the grave.

In John 10:28, Jesus says,

> *"I give them eternal life, and they will never perish. No one can snatch them away from me."*

God offers you a clean slate and a fresh new start with Him. When we place our faith in Jesus Christ, everything becomes new (2 Corinthians 5:17).

God desires an everlasting relationship with us in which we are His beloved children and He is our loving Heavenly Father. He wants to walk hand in hand with us through this life, and ultimately spend eternity with us.

Have you surrendered to the awesome gift of Salvation?

If so, I pray this chapter serves as a reminder of how amazing the Architect's design for Salvation is.

I pray that your heart is stirred with the reality that many have not heard this lifechanging message of hope, and God is eager for you to share it with others!

If you have not yet placed your faith in Christ, I want to encourage you to take the time now to seek Him.

He already knows exactly where you are and what you're going through. He knows your needs, your faults, and your failures.

He loves you, and has gone to great lengths to make it possible for you to know Him.

Simply place your faith in Christ, acknowledging that you are a sinner, but believing that He paid the price for your sins so you can experience forgiveness, newness of life, and an eternal relationship with a loving God.

Who You Are

As we close out this chapter I want to share with you some powerful lyrics from one of my favorite Christian artists, Unspoken. In their song "Who You Are," we find these encouraging words:

I know that look you're giving, like you've got something to prove
'Cause I have walked for miles and miles in that same pair of shoes
You refuse forgiveness like it's something to be earned
Sometimes pain's the only way that we can learn

You believe in freedom, but you don't know how to choose
You've got to step out of your feelings that you're so afraid to lose
And every day you put your feet on the floor,
You've got to walk through the door
It's never gonna be easy but it's all worth fighting for

So let the ashes fall wherever they land
Come back from wherever you've been
To the foot of the Cross,
To the feet of Jesus, the feet of Jesus

You can never fall too hard, so fast, so far
That you can't get back when you're lost
Where you are is never too late, so bad, so much
That you can't change
You can change who you are.

The Building Blocks
QUESTIONS ADDITIONAL STUDY APPLICATION

Thoughts from Chapter 2: The Breath and the Barrier

The average adult breathes 12-18 times per minute, and up to 70 times per minute while under extreme stress or exercise. But physicians tell us that the optimum rhythm for breathing is 3-4 breaths per minute. When stress, anxiety, and fear make you breath hard, it is ultimately caused by sin. Jesus Christ paid the price for your sins, experiencing the death you deserved. For three days in the grave He was without the breath of life. The same breath of God that breathed perfect life into Adam resurrected Jesus Christ from the grave, giving you victory over sin. The same breath of God that raised Jesus Christ from the dead also resurrects your spirit so you can breathe easy, resting in the presence of a loving God.

Questions to Consider

Can you remember a specific time when you placed your faith in Jesus Christ, confessing that He died for your sins? Can you give a testimony of your Salvation?

Read 1 John 5:11-13. Do you have assurance of your Salvation? Do you ever struggle with doubt? If so, why?

What are some things in life that cause you stress, worry, or fear?

Does the stress of this world suffocate your faith, or are you able to rest in the assurance of your Salvation?

What are some things you can do on a daily basis to remind yourself of how awesome the gift of Salvation is?

Additional Verses to Study / How Can i Apply This?

- Romans 8:11, 31-39

- Luke 8:4-15

- Luke 8:4-15

- John 10:1-30

- Isaiah 53

- 1 Peter 1:3-12

Building Blocks: Before i Move On...

☐ I can give a testimony of my Salvation through Jesus Christ.

☐ Even though I sometimes experience stress, anxiety, and fear in this life, I am able to rest in the assurance of my Salvation.

☐ I am not perfect. My salvation doesn't depend on my ability to be perfect, but rather on Christ's perfect power perfecting me.

☐ I understand that Salvation is just the beginning. I am hungry to grow.

Prayer

Heavenly Father, I praise you for the awesome gift of Salvation. I am so thankful that You sent Your Son to pay the price I couldn't pay, so I could be forgiven and experience a relationship with You. Help me to firmly establish the building block of Salvation in my life so my faith will never be shaken by feelings of doubt or worry. Give me the boldness to share my Salvation testimony so others may hear of Your great mercy and love. Help me to grow and experience a faith that is full and complete. Amen.

CHAPTER 3
IDENTITY

> *This means that anyone who belongs to Christ has become a new person. The old life is gone; a new life has begun!*
>
> *2 Corinthians 5:17*

You are not who you once were. You have a new identity.

Sin once defined who you were – a sinner lost and without hope, separated from God, and living only by your own ambitions and desires. You are now a citizen of Heaven – a sinner saved by grace, fully redeemed.

Although we continue to live in the same world, it is critical to realize that in Christ we are not who we once were. The plan of Salvation was written by a God of grace and mercy. God is rich in His passion for new beginnings. When we accept Jesus Christ as our Redeemer, we are reborn into a new life in Christ.

During the days of Jesus' ministry on the earth, there was a religious leader named Nicodemus. We don't know a lot about him, but we do know that he held Jesus in high regard. Not only did Nicodemus acknowledge Jesus' power and divinity, he wanted to understand the truths of His teachings. Jesus told him there was a spiritual transformation he needed before he could fully understand. Nicodemus needed a new beginning.

Jesus said in John 3:3,

> *I tell you the truth, unless you are born again, you cannot see the Kingdom of God.*

Nicodemus was a religious leader, a student of the scrolls and manuscripts. He knew God's law, as recorded in the Old Testament, and had a desire to learn more. On all accounts Nicodemus was a good man, and yet, Jesus said he must be born again. Nicodemus struggled with this idea.

In John 3:6-8 Jesus continued by saying,

> *Humans can reproduce only human life, but the Holy Spirit gives birth to spiritual life. So don't be surprised when I say, 'You must be born again.' The wind blows wherever it wants. Just as you can hear the wind but can't tell where it comes from or where it is going, so you can't explain how people are born of the Spirit.*

Faith in Christ is the starting point for a supernatural new beginning in life. This lifechange is so radical it's like being born a second time. It's the transition from being a child of darkness to a child of brilliant light. The Holy Spirit literally changes our identity.

The old is gone and the new has come. Our sins are removed from us as far as the east is from the west (Psalm 103:12). If you have placed your faith in Christ, you are now a born-again believer in the Savior of the world. Your life will never be the same. In fact, your life as you knew it just ended.

A new life awaits.

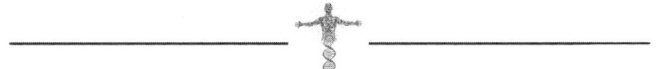

The Gumball Machine

If you've ever been to a shopping mall, you know that one of the main attractions for kids are the vending machines that sell gumballs and candy. This oasis of fun is usually located right at the center of the mall so no one will miss it. When a child fixes their eyes on a gumball, that's all they care about. My kids know that a quarter is all that stands between them and the sweet flavored prize on the other side of the glass.

"Can I have quarter? Can I? Can I? Please can I have a quarter? Pleeeeeeease....?" This is the universal plea of kids everywhere.

The gumball is the prize. A quarter is all they need to get it.

In that moment, my kids simply want a gumball. They don't care what I'm wearing. They don't care what car I drive. They don't care how smart

I am or whether or not I have a degree. They don't care if I make $10 a year or $100,000 a year.

They just want a gumball.

I could hand them a hundred dollar bill and they would hand it back. I could hand them a dime, a nickel, a penny, a half-dollar, or a subway token, and they would hand each one back.

Only a quarter is the right shape and size to unlock the mechanical gear that turns to release a gumball. It's that simple. In that moment, to them, a quarter is worth more than gold.

What are you worth?

Over the years I've answered this question in various ways. As a child, my worth rested on my parent's approval. In high school, it revolved around my looks and popularity. At other times my worth was determined by how much money I made.

Society loves to judge the value of things and people. Hollywood does a tremendous job of developing an ever-changing currency of beauty and sex appeal. Corporate America is continually redefining the benchmark of success. People constantly measure themselves up against one another. The "standard" of success is set so high that no one can possibly attain it. Even the wealthiest, most successful business people feel like they don't earn enough. The most beautiful individuals feel ugly compared to the standard of perfection that society puts before them.

Just think about all the reality TV shows that judge contestants on their intelligence, talent, or beauty. No matter how good people are, they're judged as inferior compared to others. Like a pool of piranhas, it's survival of the fittest. We live in a world of materialism. It's boastful, judgmental, and dangerously demeaning.

How do you measure your worth? As a child, did you feel rejected by your parents? Have you felt like a failure in your career? Has a crumbling marriage left you feeling unwanted or devalued?

You are the quarter. Your relationship with God is the gumball. Salvation is the mechanical coin slot that makes it all work.

All He wants is you.

God doesn't care about your monetary value or how you stack up against *People* magazine's top 100 hot bodies. He doesn't judge you by the degrees you earn, the job title you hold, or the awards you win.

He loves you for you.

You are perfectly designed for a passionate relationship.

He created you. He paid a great price for you. You are precious and beautiful in His sight. The truth of His love should fill us with confidence and dispel all feelings of failure or inadequacy. No matter how other people judge you, your true worth is found in the arms of a relentless, pursuing God who holds eternity in His hands.

You may be nothing to this world, but you are everything to Him. Stop defining yourself by what other people think about you, and start defining yourself by what God thinks about you.

Our new life in Christ redefines everything we thought about worth and promises us a place of royalty.

Welcome To The Family

> *But to all who believed him and accepted him, he gave the right to become children of God.*
>
> *John 1:12*

You are a child of God.

Think about that. You are a child of the grand Architect, and He is your Father. This is a crucial truth for every Christian. Whether you recently embraced Christ as your personal Savior or you have been a Christian for years – your new identity starts with your adoption into the Family of God.

Our Heavenly Father is limitless in His love and pursuit of us. He is the Creator of the galaxies, the Shaper of the earth, and the One who knows the very number of hairs on your head. He orchestrates your life, navigating you through the plots of sin and redeeming you through the blood of His only Son. You are adopted. You are an heir to His Kingdom. You are His child.

We were born as sinners and our spirit was dead in trespasses. When we place our faith in Jesus Christ, we are not only reconciled to the Father, but the Holy Spirit renovates our lives. By God's Blueprinted design, our spirit is born with a newness of life in Christ.

> *And because we are his children, God has sent the Spirit of his Son into our hearts, prompting us to call out, "Abba, Father."*
>
> *Galatians 4:6*
>
> *So you have not received a spirit that makes you fearful slaves. Instead, you received God's Spirit when he adopted you as his own children. Now we call him, "Abba, Father."*
>
> *Romans 8:15*

God desires to have an intimate relationship with you. He's not calling you His child as a formality. He adopts you into His family because He wants you. The word "Abba" is used by Jewish children to address their father. It's like the English word "dad."

God is literally your Heavenly Dad.

He wants to talk to you every day. He wants to share in your laughs, your struggles, your victories, and your tears. He whole-heartedly understands that you are going to falter and yet He declares His patience and grace. Like a father who teaches his child to walk, ride a bike, balance a checkbook, and become an adult – God is committed to every aspect of your walk with Him.

God is not some distant, abstract figure. God is right here, right now. He is your best friend and He wants you to embrace your place as His child.

You are not a failure. You are so much more than you ever thought you could be. You have a Dad who is all-knowing, all-powerful, and above all things. Your Dad is the beginning and the end, and His love for you is more than you will ever realize.

Cast off those regrets. Embrace the awesome Blueprint of God's priceless love. Deny Satan's attempts to haunt your mind with your shortfalls. Square those shoulders and declare your place in the Family of God. Stop searching for worth, and realize that the One who is limitless in His riches calls you His child – His priceless jewel.

Brothers

For God knew his people in advance, and he chose them to become like his Son, so that his Son would be the firstborn among many brothers and sisters.

Romans 8:29

You are designed to be like Christ.

Romans 8 is one of my favorite passages of Scripture. We have a spiritual DNA that begins to take shape as we discover our place as a child of God. He designed the Blueprint of redemption not only to save us, but to transform us into the image of His Son.

God calls you to become like Christ. He wants all His children to grow into the image of His Son. It's as natural as a baby learning to crawl. It's as intentional as a toddler learning to walk. God wants you to grow in your faith. As you grow, your identity will point others to the Cross.

I'm reminded of my relationship with my younger brother Tyran. There are six years between us, yet we always managed to spend a ton of time together growing up. We had a great relationship. He went to my basketball practices and asked the coach if he could practice too. It wasn't long before Ty was a walking stat book from hours of conversations and studying professional players from the NBA. We collected basketball cards together and watched countless games on TV.

If I learned a new move, he would practice for hours until he got it. When I got up early to go to the courts, he went with me. I loved basketball, so he loved basketball. I practiced, so he practiced. I played, so he played. I was the big brother and he was on a quest to be like me.

Jesus Christ is our big brother, and He's already set the ultimate example for us to follow. Romans 8:29 is an invitation for us to look to Christ not only as our Savior, but also as a brother who welcomes us to walk at His side.

I often ask myself if my desire to be like Christ is equal to the desire Ty had to be like me. Do I have that same kind of passionate commitment to be His reflection?

The word "firstborn" in this verse can also be translated as *supreme*. The enemy is desperately trying to stop us from living radically under the supremacy of Jesus. Why? Because a life fully surrendered to the authority of the Savior changes the world.

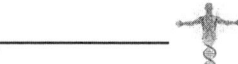

Light

You are the light of the world—like a city on a hilltop that cannot be hidden. No one lights a lamp and then puts it under a basket. Instead, a lamp is placed on a stand, where it gives light to everyone in the house. In the same way, let your good deeds shine out for all to see, so that everyone will praise your heavenly Father.

Matthew 5:14-16

After years of anticipation and proclamation, Jesus stood on a mountaintop and delivered His first sermon recorded in Scripture. No one was prepared for His bold and challenging words.

In that day, the Pharisees were gaudy, robe-wearing, holier-than-thou religious leaders. They were prideful, judgmental, and legalistic. The majority of the people were never encouraged to teach, lead, or publicly minister to others. Only the smartest students, the upper echelon of men, could obtain rabbi status. This led to great religious abuse.

In defiance of the religious authorities, Jesus began to call ordinary fishermen to be His disciples (Matthew 4:18-20). The Pharisees watched as poor, uneducated people began to teach, preach, and make disciples. Jesus didn't teach the powerful and the successful. He specifically sought out the poor, sick, and rejected. He ministered to tax collectors, lepers, and prostitutes. He healed the diseased, lifted up the downtrodden, and empowered the weak. He took the people society calls "failures" and transformed them into the lights of the world.

No matter who you are or where you come from, if you've placed your faith in Jesus Christ, you are the light of the world.

Have you embraced that identity? Are you ready to live it out in everyday life?

Less Talk, More Action

Many Christians spend hours delving into deep theological study. They study the locations, customs, methods, languages, writing styles, and cross-references of the Bible. We get so caught up in the technical nuances of Scripture that we too easily forget about the earth-shaking truths found in the simplicity of God's Word. This is a big problem.

Don't get me wrong. I believe there are many Christians who earnestly desire to know God's Word in great depth. They read God's Word with the purest of hearts and desire to study to show themselves approved (2 Timothy 2:15). That's biblical.

However, it's easy to spend way too much time studying complex passages and having in-depth discussions on "gray areas." We will spend hours talking about tattoos, maybe even days. Yet, most will never embrace the simple command to love God with all their hearts. Why do we do this? Is it because in the simplest passages we find the most conviction? Have we convinced ourselves that our mastering of peripheral topics makes us appear more "holy" to an all-knowing God?

The devil has done an effective job convincing us that truth proclaimed in one sentence can't be as important as a topic that intrigues us for hours of conversation. Don't let the simplicity of being "light" fool you. It's in God's Word for a great purpose and we can't allow ourselves to miss it.

Our youngest child was born December 19, 2009. Soon after his delivery I watched as nurses took Karter – now just a few minutes old – and placed him under a heat lamp to keep him warm. With the warmth of the light shining down on him, I watched as he stretched and opened his little eyes. With just a squint, Karter took in a whole new world. Imagine what that must be like to catch a glimpse of light for the first time.

Exhilarating. Freeing. Moving.

At Creation, God spoke light into existence and He separated it from darkness. Over 1,500 years after Moses recorded Genesis through the divine inspiration of God, we see this separation in the flesh. We see it take spiritual shape. The Apostle John writes this about Jesus:

> *In the beginning the Word already existed. The Word was with God, and the Word was God. He existed in the beginning with God. God created everything through him, and nothing was created except through him. The Word gave life to everything that was created, and his life brought light to everyone. The light shines in the darkness, and the darkness can never extinguish it. God sent a man, John the Baptist, to tell about the light so that everyone might believe because of his testimony. John himself was not the light; he was simply a witness to tell about the light. The one who is the true light, who gives light to everyone, was coming into the world. He came into the very world he created, but the world didn't recognize him. He came to his own people, and even they rejected him. But to all who believed him and accepted him, he gave the right to become children of God. They are reborn—not with a physical birth resulting from human passion or plan, but a birth that comes from God.*
>
> *John 1:1-13*

"He came into the very world he created, but the world didn't recognize him." I like how John comes right out with this awesome truth. He doesn't pull any punches. This is a truth that should convict and lead us to be more of what God calls us to be.

Jesus is Light. When He came on the scene, all those living in darkness simply didn't get it at first. Darkness and Jesus are like oil and water, hot and cold, chocolate and vanilla. Jesus was different. He stuck out. He taught people a new way of living that's the exact opposite of the norm.

In an effort to make Christianity trendy and relevant, many churches have watered-down the gospel message into something culturally acceptable, non-confrontational, and tolerant of sin.

We are called to be different. There must be a difference between us and those Jesus called us to shine on. But we've mastered the art of straddling the fence. We want to feel "spiritual," yet maintain our cultural status of being relevant and accepted by the secular world.

We go to church on Sunday and read our Bibles, but to the world looking on we are not much different than they are. We have "heroically" taken on the task of making God faithlessly comprehensible to the lost – an effort we were never called to tackle.

Does your life reflect a love-stricken light that reveals the need for a Savior?

Light is powerful. Light is supernatural. Light is different. You are light.

Deliberately Different

Jesus' Sermon on the Mount (Matthew 5-7) contains some truly amazing words. When He preached this sermon in front of thousands of people, His breath Blueprinted a life of being radically different:

> *God blesses those who are poor and realize their need for him, for the Kingdom of Heaven is theirs.*

God blesses those who mourn, for they will be comforted.

God blesses those who are humble, for they will inherit the whole earth.

God blesses those who hunger and thirst for justice, for they will be satisfied.

God blesses those who are merciful, for they will be shown mercy.

God blesses those whose hearts are pure, for they will see God.

God blesses those who work for peace, for they will be called the children of God.

God blesses those who are persecuted for doing right, for the Kingdom of Heaven is theirs.

God blesses you when people mock you and persecute you and lie about you and say all sorts of evil things against you because you are followers. Be happy about it! Be very glad! For a great reward awaits you in heaven. And remember, the ancient prophets were persecuted in the same way.

But I say, if you are even angry with someone, you are subject to judgment! If you call someone an idiot, you are in danger of being brought before the court.

But I say, anyone who even looks at a woman with lust has already committed adultery with her in his heart.

But I say, do not resist an evil person! If someone slaps you on the right cheek, offer the other cheek also. If you are sued in court and your shirt is taken from you, give your coat, too.

But I say, love your enemies! Pray for those who persecute you! In that way, you will be acting as true children of your Father in heaven. For he gives his sunlight to both the evil and the good, and he sends rain on the just and the unjust alike. If you love only those who love you, what reward is there for that? Even corrupt tax collectors do that much. If you are kind only to your friends, how are you different from anyone else? Even pagans do that. But you are to be perfect, even as your Father in heaven is perfect.

Watch out! Don't do your good deeds publicly, to be admired by others, for you will lose the reward from your Father in heaven.

If you forgive those who sin against you, your heavenly Father will forgive you. But if you refuse to forgive others, your Father will not forgive your sins.

You cannot serve both God and money.

That is why I tell you not to worry about everyday life— whether you have enough food and drink, or enough clothes to wear. Isn't life more than food, and your body more than clothing?

Do not judge others, and you will not be judged. For you will be treated as you treat others.

Yes, just as you can identify a tree by its fruit, so you can identify people by their actions.

Excerpts from Matthew 5-7

Jesus focuses on the true condition of the heart and makes it very clear that to be light, we must be different. His message is one of radical peacemaking, forgiveness, and sacrifice.

Love is the wattage that powers the light of our testimony.

Being a Christian has nothing to do with religion. It's not about traditions or formalities. It's not about rituals or rules. It's not about Sunday. It's not about going to church or sitting in a pew. It's not about hearing sermons. It's not even about reading the Bible.

Being a Christian means being different. It's an active faith of doing.

Being light is more than just glowing in the dark and priding ourselves in being different from the darkness. Truly shining as the light of the world means actively penetrating the darkness and transforming it through the power of relentless love.

It means living in a way that makes the world stop and wonder. It's about going above and beyond the societal norms.

It means turning the other cheek when the world tells you to punch back.

It means giving away your coat when the world says to take as much as you can get.

It means going the extra mile when you have no obligation to do so.

It's crazy. But it's crazy enough to change the world.

Savior-Separate

Many Christians make too much sense. This may sound odd, but I believe many Christians are too normal and earthly-minded. Christians must move from being earthly-minded to being spiritually-minded. The Apostle Paul (originally called "Saul") writes in Romans 12:2,

> *Don't copy the behavior and customs of this world, but let God transform you into a new person by changing the way you think. Then you will learn to know God's will for you, which is good and pleasing and perfect.*

Imagine a "good Christian." Paul was originally the opposite. He was far from holy. In fact, before coming to Christ, he arrested Christians and had them executed. It wasn't until He was on the road to Damascus that he encountered the great Light that revealed the darkness he was in and changed him forever. Acts 9:3-4 says:

> *As he was approaching Damascus on this mission, a light from heaven suddenly shone down around him. He fell*

> *to the ground and heard a voice saying to him, "Saul! Saul! Why are you persecuting me?"*

After Paul's conversion, his ministry began. That in itself is incredible. Only God in His amazing ability to transform lives could take a Christian-persecutor and turn him into a Christian leader. In the early stages of Paul's ministry, Christians were skeptical of him. After all, this was the same man who had tried to kill them. Acts 9:26-27 reads,

> *When Saul arrived in Jerusalem, he tried to meet with the believers, but they were all afraid of him. They did not believe he had truly become a believer! Then Barnabas brought him to the apostles and told them how Saul had seen the Lord on the way to Damascus and how the Lord had spoken to Saul. He also told them that Saul had preached boldly in the name of Jesus in Damascus.*

Barnabas used the phrase "preached boldly" when describing Paul. A few of the definitions of "bold" are "fearless," "to stand out," and "prominent." I can imagine what some of Paul's old supporters must have said after Paul began his ministry. "He's lost it." "He doesn't make any sense to me." "He's different!"

A halfhearted, under-the-surface change would never have been enough for Paul to do as he did. It had to be very bold, drastic, and even incomprehensible.

Paul writes that we must not be conformed to this world, but be radically changed in the way we think. We have to stop trying to make sense to the world and start being Savior-Separate.

"Savior-Separate" is a term I came up with to help define the difference between being separate from the world in order to look religious, and being separate for the purpose of following Christ. Being Savior-Separate demonstrates your faith to others so you can bring glory to God.

When we are Savior-Separate, God uses us in a supernatural way to change the world. He takes our bold distinction and, through the power of the Holy Spirit, uses us to reveal Christ.

We need to be different from this world if we want to follow Him.

Let's be honest, most of us desire the easy road. Being different means standing out. Being bold in our pursuit of Christ may mean facing adversity or slander.

Being Savior-Separate requires sacrifice.

But Peter writes:

> *But even if you suffer for doing what is right, God will reward you for it. So don't worry or be afraid of their threats. Remember, it is better to suffer for doing good, if that is what God wants, than to suffer for doing wrong!*
>
> 1 Peter 3:14, 17

Truthfully, although this is encouraging, it doesn't make me want to run out and find the best way to suffer for Jesus. Our culture doesn't make it easy to follow Christ. We are surrounded by distractions and comforts. We are encouraged to stay up with the latest trends, fashion, technology, and entertainment. It's a fast-moving world and everyone's watching to see who fits in, who's the next trendsetter, who's on top. We're a bunch of self-trained glory addicts and Jesus is nothing more than the afterthought we get on Sunday afternoon when our favorite player scores a touchdown and points to the Heavens on our 50-inch 3D LED HDTV with backlighting.

Suffer? Who wants to suffer?

Yet, despite all of society's worldly thinking, we are called to be Christ-like. We are called to place God's Word at the center of our hearts and live it out in our lives as if God Himself was counting on it. There will be times when this will push us to the edge. We will be tested. We may fail. But we should find great peace and joy from the truth found in 1 Peter 3:14-17 because we are living it. We are shining.

This process of becoming more like Christ does not happen overnight. It takes patience, humility, and discipline.

Sin screams "self," but God whispers "Savior."

The Early Christians

I want to close out this chapter by sharing with you some powerful words from the Letter to Diognetus. This is a real historical document written in the second century A.D. for the purpose of defending Christianity. It was written to Diognetus, a tutor of Emperor Marcus Aurelius. This letter is historical proof that early Christians lived in such a countercultural way that the world was moved to take notice. The letter reads:

> *For Christians cannot be distinguished from the rest of the human race by country or language or customs. They do not live in cities of their own; they do not use a peculiar form of speech; they do not follow an eccentric manner of life. This doctrine of theirs has not been discovered by the ingenuity or deep thought of inquisitive men, nor do they put forward a merely human teaching, as some people do. Yet, although they live in Greek and barbarian cities alike, as each man's lot has been cast, and follow the customs of the country in clothing and food and other matters of daily living, at the same time they give proof of the remarkable and admittedly extraordinary constitution of their own commonwealth. They live in their own countries, but only as aliens. They have a share in everything as citizens, and endure everything as foreigners. Every foreign land is their fatherland, and yet for them every fatherland is a foreign land. They marry, like everyone else, and they beget children, but they do not cast out their offspring. They share their board with each other, but not their marriage bed. It is true that they are "in the flesh," but they do not live "according to the flesh." They busy themselves on earth, but their citizenship is in heaven. They obey the established laws, but in their own lives they go far beyond what the laws require. They love all men, and by all men they are persecuted. They are unknown, and still they are condemned; they are put to death, and yet they are brought to life. They are poor, and yet they make many*

> rich; they are completely destitute, and yet they enjoy complete abundance.

As early as the second century, Christians already had a reputation of being Savior-Separate. The more they embraced their identity as children of God and endeavored to follow Christ, the more they became like Christ. Remember how my brother Ty would spend hours practicing basketball because he wanted to be like me? By the age of ten, Ty already had a reputation in our town of being a phenomenal basketball player. He was too young and too small to play on high school teams, yet high school players welcomed him to participate. They wanted to play with him and see his skills with their own eyes. Nobody looked down on him because of his age, his height, his looks, his clothing, his wiry spiked hair, his neon green shoelaces, or his ninja turtle nunchucks. He pursued my leading, grew in big brother imagery, and developed a reputation that transcended the boundaries. I hope you grasp these next words of encouragement.

The more you become like Christ, the less important your imperfections become.

I have all kinds of issues. I'm impatient. I struggle with compassion. My wife says I yell when I talk. I shave between my eyebrows. I am partial to sweater vests, yet I enjoy riding my Harley (an embarrassing combination!). Every day, I shake my head and ask God, "How in the world can You use me? I'm a mess!"

But that's the beauty of it! God doesn't always choose the most talented, most beautiful, or most holy people. He chooses imperfect, broken, needy people, and through His grace He transforms them. As you surrender to the Blueprint, He will break boundaries you never thought were possible. He does extraordinary things with ordinary people. God's mercy is greater than our sin. God's Blueprint is infused with the full knowledge of our shortfalls. His patience remains through our growing pains. His mercy transforms our failures into testimonies of His glory. Paul writes in 1 Timothy 1:12-17,

> I thank Christ Jesus our Lord, who has given me strength to do his work. He considered me trustworthy and appointed me to serve him, even though I used to blaspheme the name of Christ. In my insolence, I

persecuted his people. But God had mercy on me because I did it in ignorance and unbelief. Oh, how generous and gracious our Lord was! He filled me with the faith and love that come from Christ Jesus.

This is a trustworthy saying, and everyone should accept it: "Christ Jesus came into the world to save sinners"— and I am the worst of them all. But God had mercy on me so that Christ Jesus could use me as a prime example of his great patience with even the worst sinners. Then others will realize that they, too, can believe in him and receive eternal life. All honor and glory to God forever and ever! He is the eternal King, the unseen one who never dies; he alone is God. Amen.

Thoughts from Chapter 3: Identity

You are not who you once were. The moment you placed your faith in Christ, everything changed. You were adopted into the Family of God. You are royalty. Your true worth is not defined by earthly standards, but by your identity as a child of God. You have a spiritual DNA designed to supernaturally transform you into the image of Christ, your spiritual big brother. The more you become like Christ, the less important your imperfections become. The more closely you walk with Christ, the more His love shines through you to illuminate a dark world. You are light. You are a worldchanger. You are called to be Savior-Separate.

Questions to Consider

What is your worth? How have you defined your worth in the past? How do you define your worth now?

Do you struggle with feelings of inadequacy? Have you fully embraced your identity as a royal child of God, His priceless jewel?

How has your life changed since being born again? How have you become more like Christ?

After reading the Sermon on the Mount in Matthew 5-7, can you identify any changes you need to make in your life to be more like Christ? What are some practical steps you can take to be deliberately different?

How is Christ's love demonstrated in your day-to-day life? Are there areas in your life where you struggle to show compassion? What are they?

Additional Verses to Study / How Can i Apply This?

- Psalm 139:1-18

- Matthew 10:28-33

- 2 Corinthians 5:17-21

- Philippians 3:20-21

- Romans 6

Building Blocks: Before i Move On...

☐ I am not who I once was. I am born again and I have new identity in Christ.

☐ I embrace God as my Heavenly Father knowing that there is nothing too big for Him to handle, and nothing too small for Him to care about.

☐ I want to activate my spiritual DNA, becoming more like Christ every day.

☐ I want to shine as the light of the world through radical compassion, exposing darkness and leading others to Christ.

Prayer

Heavenly Father, I praise you for adopting me into Your family. What an awesome privilege it is to be able to call You my Heavenly Dad! Please help me to forget my old life and live completely for You. Inspire and empower me to be the light You desire me to be, reaching others for Christ through acts of compassion, mercy, and love. Help me to embrace my identity as a child of God and an ambassador for Christ. Amen.

CHAPTER 4
FILLED

> *"But you will receive power when the Holy Spirit comes upon you. And you will be my witnesses, telling people about me everywhere—in Jerusalem, throughout Judea, in Samaria, and to the ends of the earth."*
>
> *After saying this, he was taken up into a cloud while they were watching, and they could no longer see him. As they strained to see him rising into heaven, two white-robed men suddenly stood among them. "Men of Galilee," they said, "why are you standing here staring into heaven? Jesus has been taken from you into heaven, but someday he will return from heaven in the same way you saw him go!"*
>
> Acts 1:8-11

"But you will receive power when the Holy Spirit comes upon you..." These were that last words Jesus said to His disciples before ascending into Heaven to sit at the right hand of the Father. Think about what that must have been like for the disciples. The eleven apostles had spent the last three years of their lives with Jesus. These are the disciples who Jesus had called, saying "follow me." They had left their families, their homes, and their jobs. They had travelled over 15,000 miles, seen the lame walk, the blind see, and the dead come to life. These were the disciples who watched Jesus multiply fishes and loaves, wither the fig tree, and speak peace over storms at sea. He was their Rabbi, their Teacher, their Lord, their Leader, their Savior, and their Friend. Jesus had spent over 1,000 days with them, and each day, the disciples were empowered by the presence of the Son of God.

I'm sure their minds went back to when Jesus said,

> *"But now I am going away to the one who sent me, and not one of you is asking where I am going. Instead, you grieve because of what I've told you. But in fact, it is best*

> *for you that I go away, because if I don't, the Advocate won't come. If I do go away, then I will send him to you."*
>
> John 16:5-7

Surely the disciples were puzzled by these words. How could it be *best* for Jesus to leave? Who is the Advocate?

When Jesus ascended into Heaven, He left the disciples with the daunting task of spreading the Gospel to the ends of the earth despite intense persecution and hatred for the message they were called to preach.

Jesus was asking them to do the impossible.

This call to change the world was one they simply couldn't do on their own. Jesus knew this. He told them at the Last Supper, "Remain in me, and I will remain in you… Apart from me you can do nothing" (John 15:4-5). Yet now Jesus had left them and gone into Heaven. Not only that, but He said it was *necessary* for Him to go away, so the Advocate could come. *Who is the Advocate?*

The Greek word translated "Advocate" is *Paraclete*. It is also translated as "Comforter," "Encourager," or "Counselor."

Think about those words.

Do you need comfort?

Do you need encouragement?

Do you need counsel?

God knew we would need a supernatural Helper. He knew we would need motivation, uplifting, wisdom, and direction.

By God's design, the Holy Spirit supernaturally seals us with His unwavering commitment and lifechanging promises.

> *It is God who enables us, along with you, to stand firm for Christ. He has commissioned us, and he has identified us as his own by placing the Holy Spirit in our hearts as the first installment that guarantees everything he has promised us.*
>
> *2 Corinthians 1:21-22*

Living by our own design instead of the leading of the Holy Spirit is the place where many Christians get stuck. We experience Salvation but often become exhausted in our own pursuit of being Savior-Separate. It's not uncommon for Christians to get lost in the journey of trying to walk as Jesus would walk.

What does it mean to follow Christ?

How do I know the right thing to do and the right words to say?

Is it really possible to live like Jesus?

How can I be Jesus to a dying world, when I'm so imperfect myself?

Do I feel alive in my faith, or empty inside?

Do I feel overwhelmed by the weight of living out my faith?

Do I feel lost and without direction?

Do I ever doubt my ability to be the person God wants me to be?

The Outpouring

After hearing the words of Jesus in Acts 1:8-11, the disciples obediently went and waited for the Advocate to come.

> *On the day of Pentecost all the believers were meeting together in one place. Suddenly, there was a sound from heaven like the roaring of a mighty windstorm, and it filled the house where they were sitting. Then, what looked like flames or tongues of fire appeared and settled on each of them. And everyone present was filled with the Holy Spirit and began speaking in other languages, as the Holy Spirit gave them this ability.*
>
> *Acts 2:1-4*

"And everyone present was filled with the Holy Spirit..." The moment the Holy Spirit fell upon the believers, everything changed. Jesus was no longer physically present, but the believers were filled with His Spirit. He sent the Holy Spirit to enable His disciples to manifest His power. This is a truly incredible gift for every believer. The believers in Acts 2 discovered firsthand the power of the Blueprint.

Our identity is shaped by our faith, but our ability to walk in it is found in the power of the Holy Spirit.

I believe the main reason believers struggle to live by the Blueprint is that they are not walking by the Spirit. Having a daily encounter with the Holy Spirit is what takes our lives from ordinary to extraordinary. Without the Holy Spirit, the early Church would have failed, and the Gospel message would have been extinguished. The call to be the light of the world, the boldness to be different, and the power to selflessly love are impossible to accomplish without the Holy Spirit empowering our lives.

Why? The Holy Spirit is the compass that navigates us through the Blueprint.

If you don't have Him, you're lost. If you're not experiencing Him, you're wandering.

The Holy Spirit is vital to your life as a parent, an employee, a pastor, a student, a disciple, a believer – a worldchanger.

Who is the Holy Spirit?

> *"But I will send you the Advocate—the Spirit of truth. He will come to you from the Father and will testify all about me."*
>
> *John 15:26*

In this verse and others, the pronoun "He" is used in reference to the Holy Spirit. This shows that the Holy Spirit is a living being, not a thing. The Holy Spirit is not an object or a representation. He is relational and His presence is personal.

> *"But you are not controlled by your sinful nature. You are controlled by the Spirit if you have the Spirit of God living in you. (And remember that those who do not have the Spirit of Christ living in them do not belong to him at all.)"*
>
> *Romans 8:9*

In Scripture, the Holy Spirit is referred to as "the Spirit of God" and "the Spirit of Christ."

The Holy Spirit is the very presence of Jesus Christ in your life!

2 Corinthians 3:17 tells us:

> *"For the Lord is the Spirit, and wherever the Spirit of the Lord is, there is freedom."*

Although there is one and only one God (Deuteronomy 6:4), God has revealed Himself in three divine "Persons": Father (Yahweh), Son (Jesus Christ), and Holy Spirit. This divine mystery that defies human comprehension is known as the "Trinity" in most Christian circles.

> *Then God said, "Let us make human beings in our image, to be like us...."*
>
> *Genesis 1:26*

"Us" – This is the first passage of scripture in which we see that God is dynamic in His very Being. Only one God, and yet, He chooses the pronoun "us!" God's vastness is greater than we can ever begin to fathom.

Consider this: Genesis 1:2 says that the Holy Spirit was involved in Creation. Hebrews 1:10 tells us that the Jesus Christ the Son *"laid the foundation of the earth and made the heavens,"* and in Isaiah 44:24, God the Father says, *"I alone stretched out the heavens."*

How is it possible for the Father to say *"I alone stretched out the heavens"* when the Son and Holy Spirit were also involved in Creation? The reality is that these three Divine "Persons" of Father, Son, and Holy Spirit are the same One God. This awesome truth is most clearly stated by Jesus Christ in Matthew 28:19, right in the middle of what's known as the "Great Commission":

> *"Therefore, go and make disciples of all the nations, baptizing them in the name of the Father and the Son and the Holy Spirit."*

Notice that Jesus did not say "in the names..." but rather, he said *"in the name...."* Three "Persons," but one name. There is only one God.... and God is the Father, God is the Son, and God is the Holy Spirit.

Is your mind blown yet? This awesome mystery humbles me every time I think about it. God is so much greater than what our little human minds are able to grasp. God cannot be put in a box or boiled down to a simple definition.

God is who He is.

God ensured your forgiveness, purpose, and eternal value through His very nature. As the Father who Blueprinted out the wonders of Creation before time began, God loves you as His very own child with a passionate and everlasting love. As the Son who carried the Cross for your sins, God is working to restore you to His family. As the Holy Spirit promised to every believer, God is eternally present with us so we can experience His Blueprint each and every day.

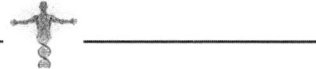

Where is the Holy Spirit?

> *And I will give you a new heart, and I will put a new spirit in you. I will take out your stony, stubborn heart and give you a tender, responsive heart. And I will put my Spirit in you so that you will follow my decrees and be careful to obey my regulations.*
>
> Ezekiel 36:26-27

God passionately desires to have a moment-by-moment relationship with you. The dynamic existence of the Holy Spirit is God's divine vehicle for drawing us to Himself and then dwelling in those who have been drawn.

The Holy Spirit is both omnipotent and omnipresent: limitless in power, knowledge, and understanding. The Spirit of God is not confined to one place at a time. Rather, He can be in all places at once. He is able to be with you, before you, and after you. He is able to be with others in the same capacity. The Holy Spirit is perfectly aware of your standing with God, the condition of your faith, and your desire for more of what God has in store for you. The Holy Spirit knows exactly where you are at this very moment. He knows your heart. He knows your longings.

Although the Holy Spirit is everywhere He desires to be, we can break "everywhere" down into two specific locations. These locations are ultimately driven by two tasks designed to bring us into our full potential in Christ.

The Drawing of the Holy Spirit: The first place we can find the Holy Spirit is *among* Creation – in the midst of people. In John 16:8, Jesus says,

> *And when he comes, he will convict the world of its sin, and of God's righteousness, and of the coming judgment.*

The Holy Spirit convicts the world of its sin. Humanity is so fallen that we are not able to come to Christ, experience Salvation, or even recognize our need for a Savior without the powerful drawing of the Holy Spirit. Each and every day, the Holy Spirit is continually guiding and directing lives, details, and circumstances to reveal to those who are lost their need for Jesus Christ. John 6:44 reads,

> *For no one can come to me unless the Father who sent me draws them to me, and at the last day I will raise them up.*

The Heavenly Father draws us back to Himself by means of the Holy Spirit convicting us of the sin that separates us from God. As we are convicted of our sin, we are able to surrender to Jesus Christ and experience forgiveness and reconciliation with God.

I am so grateful for the Holy Spirit's faithfulness in my life. I can recall times as a child when God came up beside me and witnessed His love and dedication to me. It was the Holy Spirit who ever so softly spoke to my heart one Sunday at church, urging me to stand up, go forward, kneel, and pray. It was the Holy Spirit who gave me an assurance of my Salvation the moment I poured my heart out to the Father and placed my faith in the Son.

The Holy Spirit has been faithful to you too. God breathed His faithfulness all over your life. However you came to know Christ, the Holy Spirit was instrumental in it. Without Him you would still be a slave to sin, captured by darkness. Praise Him. Thank Him. Get lost in the humbling reality that God has called you by name.

If you still aren't sure where you stand with God, I encourage you to pause before God and ask the Holy Spirit to witness to you right now. If you can't remember a time when you humbled yourself before God and placed your faith in the Savior of the world, allow the Presence of God to move upon you and draw you to repentance. Follow Him as He leads you to the foot of the Cross.

He draws us so we can declare Him.

The Dwelling of the Holy Spirit: The moment we place our faith in Christ, the Holy Spirit dwells in us. If there is one thing I pray you fully grasp about God's Blueprint it is this: *Through the Holy Spirit, God lives in you!*

The very breath of Creation, the very Spirit that filled the early church at Pentecost – He is in you. You are Spirit filled!

> *Don't you realize that your body is the temple of the Holy Spirit, who lives in you and was given to you by God? You do not belong to yourself, for God bought you with a high price. So you must honor God with your body.*
>
> *1 Corinthians 6:19-20*

In the Old Testament, God gave specific instructions for the children of Israel to construct a tabernacle. Inside that tabernacle was a specific place called the "Holy of Holies." The Holy of Holies was a place that only the High Priest could enter, and even he could only enter it once a year. It was the place where the Presence of God was found. There were specific instructions given to the High Priest for entering such a glorious place (Leviticus 16:2-10). Clothing of royalty, sacrifice, and the purest of actions were required to enter the place where God dwelled.

As we fast-forward to Jesus Christ's death on the Cross we find an incredible event that perfectly coincides with our Savior's sacrifice. Mark 15:37-38 declares,

> *Then Jesus uttered another loud cry and breathed his last. And the curtain in the sanctuary of the Temple was torn in two, from top to bottom.*

This was the curtain that separated the Holy of Holies from the rest of the Temple. When Jesus Christ died He became the last and final sacrifice needed to dwell in the Presence of God. The veil was torn and all those who are believers in Christ literally become the new Holy of Holies in which the Holy Spirit dwells. Jesus Christ's death and resurrection made a way for us to experience a moment-by-moment encounter with the breath of God. This is not a small matter. This huge, lifechanging gift encompasses all of who we are.

What Does the Holy Spirit Do?

When the Spirit of truth comes, he will guide you into all truth. He will not speak on his own but will tell you what he has heard. He will tell you about the future. He will bring me glory by telling you whatever he receives from me. All that belongs to the Father is mine; this is why I said, 'The Spirit will tell you whatever he receives from me.'

John 16:13-15

When we share Christ's message with others, we bring glory to Him. Similarly, what the Holy Spirit communicates to us comes from Jesus Christ, and glorifies Him. Through the Holy Spirit, Jesus Christ *personally* disciples us!

For God wanted them to know that the riches and glory of Christ are for you Gentiles, too. And this is the secret: Christ lives in you. This gives you assurance of sharing his glory.

Colossians 1:27

Jesus sent the Spirit so we can experience true discipleship and become fully equipped to share with others the riches we have received as part of our adoption into the family of God. The Holy Spirit works in us by optimizing the ministry of Christ through teaching, praying, and leading. If you are not fully in tune with what the Holy Spirit can do in your life, you are missing out on the completeness of God's plan for you.

When a potter molds and shapes a piece of pottery from clay, he or she spends hours perfectly shaping each piece for its intended use. Once the piece is complete, it's placed in a kiln to be heated and dried. During that process, pieces often develop cracks or blemishes that need to be filled in. The potter heats up wax and melts it over the areas of concern, smoothing them out and covering them over with clay to achieve an acceptable finished product. However, every once in a while, a piece comes out of the kiln perfectly formed with no blemishes or cracks, exactly as the potter intended. Without wax, it's ready to be set aside to fulfill its special purpose according to its design.

God is the Potter; we are the clay. Without Him, we are like a lump of clay with no specific purpose. But when God molds us into a beautiful and useful vessel, we can live according to His design. God's Blueprint is to mold you into the perfect vessel He desires you to be – a vessel "without wax" that not only holds His blessings, but also pours out His blessings to others by sharing the Good News of Christ (Galatians 3:8). The Holy Spirit is the Potter's way of achieving this work in you. He doesn't just cover up your imperfections with wax, but fundamentally transforms you into an authentic image of Christ.

The Holy Spirit Teaches: The primary way the Potter molds us into the vessels He desires us to be is through His Word – both His written Word (the Bible) and His spoken word (revelation by the Holy Spirit).

> *For the word of God is alive and powerful. It is sharper than the sharpest two-edged sword, cutting between soul and spirit, between joint and marrow. It exposes our innermost thoughts and desires.*
>
> *Hebrews 4:12*

The Bible is not a book authored by man. It is the very essence of Truth, alive and powerfully transforming us. The word "word" in this passage is translated from the Greek word *logos*, defined as "a decree, mandate, or order." The Bible is a divine expression breathed by God and given to us by the inspiration of the Holy Spirit.

> *Above all, you must realize that no prophecy in Scripture ever came from the prophet's own understanding, or from human initiative. No, those prophets were moved by the Holy Spirit, and they spoke from God.*
>
> *2 Peter 1:20-21*

Having a real understanding of the Bible is not just for pastors or church leaders. 2 Timothy 2:15 tells us that we should study to show ourselves approved. Paul tells Timothy – a new believer – to correctly interpret and explain the Word of Truth.

God is the Architect, and the Bible is His Blueprint. We are the workers commissioned with the task of building His Kingdom. We've been given the Blueprint, but we need the Architect's personal direction and guidance to fully understand and implement it in our lives. Jesus gave us the Holy Spirit to help us fully accomplish the call to study, interpret, and teach others the Scriptures. Jesus said:

> *But when the Father sends the Advocate as my representative—that is, the Holy Spirit—he will teach you everything and will remind you of everything I have told you.*
>
> *John 14:26*

As we read the Bible daily with open hearts, the Holy Spirit teaches us and reminds us of Christ's words, allowing Jesus Christ to disciple us as we study. He also teaches us through divine revelation – navigating us through the Blueprint in real time.

Jesus was led by the Holy Spirit into the wilderness, where He ate nothing for forty days and nights. He must have been extremely hungry, but He understood that being spiritually fed by God's Word is more important than having a full stomach.

> *Then Jesus was led by the Spirit into the wilderness to be tempted there by the devil. For forty days and forty nights he fasted and became very hungry. During that time the devil came and said to him, "If you are the Son of God, tell these stones to become loaves of bread."*
>
> *But Jesus told him, "No! The Scriptures say, 'People do not live by bread alone but by every word that comes from the mouth of God.'"*
>
> Matthew 4:1-4

The word "word" in this passage is translated from the Greek word *rhema*. *Rhema* refers to the spoken word – God's personal voice communicating with us through the Holy Spirit.

> *Your own ears will hear him. Right behind you a voice will say, "This is the way you should go," whether to the right or to the left.*
>
> Isaiah 30:21

Christ's answer to Satan, *"People do not live by bread alone but by every word [rhema] that comes from the mouth of God,"* is telling us that the spiritual revelation of God – His daily instruction through the Holy Spirit – is even more important than physical food. Every step Jesus took was guided by the Holy Spirit and in perfect harmony with the will of the Father. The personal guidance the Holy Spirit provides in our lives is critically important. It is the spiritual food that sustains us.

> *Like newborn babies, you must crave pure spiritual milk so that you will grow into a full experience of salvation. Cry out for this nourishment, now that you have had a taste of the Lord's kindness.*
>
> 1 Peter 2:2-3

Jesus Christ sent you the Holy Spirit so He could minister to you, mold you, shape you, and strengthen you in your daily walk. If you're depending on your pastor or life coach to do that for you, you're missing out on the fullness of God's plan for your life. Pastors have a biblical call to teach the Word, but every believer is called to apply and live the Word through direction from the Holy Spirit.

Don't rely on this book to give you all the answers either!

This book is about God's Blueprint, but this book is not the Blueprint. To read the real Blueprint, open your Bible and ask God to give you correct understanding of what you read through the Holy Spirit working within you.

Is the Holy Spirit teaching you each day? Are you being discipled by Jesus Christ? Power is found in God's written and spoken Word.

Although the enemy will try to distract you and keep you busy, nothing will substitute time spent under the tutelage of the Savior of the World.

> *When I discovered your words, I devoured them. They are my joy and my heart's delight, for I bear your name, O LORD God of Heaven's Armies.*
>
> *Jeremiah 15:16*

The Holy Spirit Prays: We have direct access to God the Father through Jesus Christ (Romans 8:34). The power of prayer is far greater than we will ever truly comprehend. God went so far as to say that we don't receive simply because we don't ask! Jesus challenges us to look at our faith when we pray. When we enter the throne room of God the Father in prayer, do we really believe that He is going to answer? So many times my prayers have been nothing more than a formality – a gesture of religiosity. But Jesus said:

> *When you pray, don't babble on and on as people of other religions do. They think their prayers are answered merely by repeating their words again and again. Don't be*

> *like them, for your Father knows exactly what you need even before you ask him!*
>
> *Matthew 6:7-8*

We should pray continually and boldly because we expect our Heavenly Father to hear and answer. Daniel prayed three times a day, every day. Abraham prayed to negotiate for God's mercy over His people. Jacob prayed for a great blessing. The prayer of Moses saved the Israelite's from God's wrath. Jonah prayed for deliverance from the belly of the great fish. Samson prayed for strength. Solomon prayed for wisdom. Story after story, account after account, we see ordinary people with great faith realizing God's power and might through prayer. God is concerned about our concerns! Prayer is a time to talk to God, share our struggles, seek His counsel, and praise Him for all He has done.

When I think about the time I spend talking to God through prayer, I'm reminded of my conversations with my own children. As their father, I love hearing them tell stories, talk about their day, laugh, and even cry when they need comfort. I certainly would not want the same exact words to come out of their mouths every day as a rote ritual. I also wouldn't want to hear from them only when they needed something. I wouldn't want them to only talk to me in a certain location or at a certain time of day. I love my kids and I want to talk to them as much as possible! I want to fulfill their needs, be there when they are hurting, and be a listening ear when they want to share something with me. I want to encourage them when they fail and applaud then when they get A's on the tests they've been studying for.

Isn't it the same way with God? If I – as an imperfect human parent – have this kind of love and desire for relationship with my children, *how much more* does Almighty God in His infinite perfection desire a relationship with His children!

He's interested in you! There is no prayer too big for Him to handle, and no prayer too small for Him to care about. You can't annoy God by praying too much. It pleases Him to hear from you! He *wants* you to pray!

So why is it that prayer seems intimidating at times? Why do we often feel like we're wasting God's time with our petty concerns? Why do we feel so unworthy to talk to God? How can it be so difficult to believe that God hears us when we pray?

If you feel unworthy when you pray, remember that you're loved by the King. A great price was paid so you could be adopted into God's Family and become His very own child.

Sometimes praying is easy and other times it's tough to even get the words out. Have you been there? Have you ever been at a place in your life when your world was dark and your circumstances seemed too intense to conquer? In those moments, we have the promise of the Holy Spirit.

It's in those challenges that we need God the most and yet we struggle for the words to pray. Amazingly, God wants the best for you so bad that the Holy Spirit prays *for you* even when you're not sure what to say. Romans 8:26 says,

> And the Holy Spirit helps us in our weakness. For example, we don't know what God wants us to pray for. But the Holy Spirit prays for us with groanings that cannot be expressed in words.

How encouraging is it to think that the Spirit of God who dwells in you is praying for you even when you don't know what to pray for, in a Heavenly language only God the Father can comprehend.

The One who created you is anointing you in prayer this very moment.

You are the temple of the Holy Spirit – a living house of prayer.

The Holy Spirit Leads: Who is leading you? I started this book sharing my testimony of coming face-to-face with this question.

The straightforward, black and white, hold-on-to-your-seat truth is this:

If the Holy Spirit isn't leading you, your life is about you and not about Jesus.

You are a child of light and therefore you are called to walk in the light. God has designed this wondrous plan of redemption to not only rescue you from the grave of sin, but also to lead you into a radical life of substance. God's will for your life has been written under the full authority of the Author. By design, His will for your life is full and complete.

The life of Christ is the ultimate example of a life led by the Spirit. Luke 4:1 declares that shortly after Christ's baptism in the Jordan River, Jesus was "full of the Holy Spirit" and "led by the Spirit." Even while Jesus was praying in the Garden of Gethsemane prior to His unlawful arrest, He prayed for the will of the Father. He was facing death, torture, the sins of the world, and the grave, and yet He sought out no other opinions or direction. He prayed, *"Your will be done"* (Matthew 26:42, Luke 22:42).

Those who do not have the Holy Spirit dwelling within them are walking through this life on their own accord. We may seek out counsel or instruction, but often that counsel is from others not living by the leading of the Spirit.

> *Oh, the joys of those who do not follow the advice of the wicked, or stand around with sinners, or join in with mockers. But they delight in the law of the LORD, meditating on it day and night. They are like trees planted along the riverbank, bearing fruit each season. Their leaves never wither, and they prosper in all they do.*
>
> *Psalm 1:1-3*

Notice this pattern of the person *not* led by the Spirit First they are following. Then they are sitting. Then they are joining. It is possible to be Spirit-filled and not Spirit-led (actively following what the Spirit guides us to do). For most believers this is a slow fade. It can be a surprisingly subtle transition from thriving under the leadership of the Architect to joining the world's quest for self-fulfillment. Paul warns the Church in Galatians 5:16,

> *But I say, walk by the Spirit, and you will not gratify the desires of the flesh.*

The day after my wife and I were married, we headed out for our honeymoon to the Pocono Mountains in Pennsylvania. I printed directions and we left from our apartment in downtown Gloversville, New York. As we approached the thruway, I didn't bother to look at the directions. I assumed I knew where the Poconos were, and headed in the direction I thought I should go. I drove two hours in the wrong direction before realizing my error. After four hours of driving, we were back where we started. Talk about a peaceful way to start off your first week of marriage! I had the directions right in front of me, but having the directions and following the directions are two different things. God presents His masterful Blueprint to us and provides the compass to navigate it, yet we often choose to blaze our own trail instead. Don't let that happen to you! If your life isn't led by the Spirit, it's built around your own desires and ambitions. That's not how it's supposed to be. We are called to fall under the AUTHORity of the Author. He is greater than "i."

The Bible calls God's sovereignty over our lives "wisdom." Wisdom is God's perfect will made known to us through the direction of the Holy Spirit. Proverbs 3:13 says,

> *Joyful is the person who finds wisdom, the one who gains understanding.*

Wisdom is joyful. Wisdom is perfect. Wisdom is crucial for the believer. The Creator knows what is absolutely best for you. His ways are straight and purposeful. Even more encouraging is this: God's wisdom is free and without expiration!

> *If you need wisdom, ask our generous God, and he will give it to you. He will not rebuke you for asking.*
>
> James 1:5

The Spirit of God is rich in overseeing all areas of your life. If you seek His instruction He will deliver it to you without rebuke or disapproval. The more we deny our flesh and cling to the Spirit, the more we experience His divine understanding of what lies ahead.

Sanctified

If we are filled with the Holy Spirit, why do we sometimes feel like God isn't with us? God is all-powerful, all-knowing, and without limitations to be all things to all believers. So why do we struggle with experiencing the strength and glory of God in our lives? Why do we often experience doubt and hesitate to share the truth of the Gospel? Why do we lack God-given attributes like joy and peace?

I love Romans 7-8. When the Apostle Paul was knee-deep in ministry, he had these same questions and troubles! The Bible is so real with us. In Romans 7, Paul ends the chapter in frustration with himself. He talks about his desire to do the right thing and his struggle with his own failures and shortcomings. He passionately wants to experience God to the fullest capacity, yet he's often left feeling empty. However, there is a great transition from Paul's struggles in chapter 7 to his anthem in Chapter 8.

> *Those who are dominated by the sinful nature think about sinful things,* **but those who are controlled by the Holy Spirit think about things that please the Spirit.** *So letting your sinful nature control your mind leads to death.* **But letting the Spirit control your mind leads to life and peace.** *For the sinful nature is always hostile to God. It never did obey God's laws, and it never will. That's why those who are still under the control of their sinful nature can never please God. But you are not controlled by your sinful nature.* **You are controlled by the Spirit if you have the Spirit of God living in you.** *(And remember that those who do not have the Spirit of Christ living in them do not belong to him at all.)*
>
> *Romans 8:5-9*

When we were slaves to sin, we became accustomed to saying "yes!" to the desires of our flesh, or sinful nature. But when we came to know

Christ, God wiped the power of sin away from us. There is no condemnation in Christ (Romans 8:1). We no longer have guilt before the throne of God the Father. Jesus Christ experienced that guilt *for us* and paid the price we could not pay.

However, Paul is telling us that we need to forsake the desires of our flesh and allow the Spirit of God to rule over us. Even though the guilt of our sins was wiped away, we still have these fallen human bodies that naturally desire sinful things. Resisting our sinful nature and responding to the Spirit's nature is a daily process of spiritual growth and discipline. The more we deny our sinful nature and surrender to the leading of the Holy Spirit, the more we experience the bountiful fruits that come from God living supremely in our lives.

This process of denying ourselves and clinging to the Spirit is called "sanctification," meaning "to be made holy – set apart for God's purpose."

> *Now may the God of peace **make you holy in every way**, and may your whole spirit and soul and body be kept blameless until our Lord Jesus Christ comes again.*
>
> 1 Thessalonians 5:23

The more the Holy Spirit reigns in your life, the more you will find yourself experiencing the joys of walking by His divinely penned instructions.

> *If you keep yourself pure, you will be a special utensil for honorable use. Your life will be clean* [sanctified], *and you will be ready for the Master to use you for every good work.*
>
> 2 Timothy 2:21

I love how Paul uses the word, "good" in this passage. In Genesis 1, when God created the universe, He said it was "good." We use the word "good" trivially, but "good" in God's eyes is magnificent beyond human comprehension! A life that is sanctified is one that lives in a moment-by-moment encounter with the Presence of God. There is nothing more powerful than being immersed in the Spirit of God.

Are you experiencing the fullness of being filled?

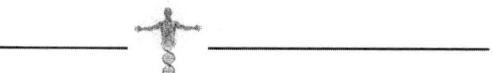

Fruity

> *But the wisdom from above is first of all pure. It is also peace loving, gentle at all times, and willing to yield to others. It is full of mercy and good deeds. It shows no favoritism and is always sincere.*
>
> James 3:17

Our lives are defined by the fruit we produce. Jesus says we are identified by it and James tells us a faith without fruit is dead. The more we seek wisdom through prayer, time in the Word, and a Spirit-led heart, the more we become rooted in a faith that flourishes and produces fruit.

The Holy Spirit's fruits are delicious to a lost world. They are captivating. To be Spirit-filled is to be fruit-filled.

> *But the Holy Spirit produces this kind of fruit in our lives: love, joy, peace, patience, kindness, goodness, faithfulness, gentleness, and self-control. There is no law against these things!*
>
> Galatians 5:22-23

The Bible teaches us that our lives should experience and radiate certain spiritual "fruits" such as love, joy, and peace. But over the years I've met many Christians who battle feelings of spiritual inadequacy they are too embarrassed to share.

As a believer, my life should be marked by the fruits of the Spirit. But for years, I lived without experiencing true love, joy, or peace in my life. I longed for a deeper relationship with God.

Notice how this passage of Scripture begins: "The Holy Spirit produces this kind of fruit in our lives..." The Holy Spirit is the provider of the things we all long for – love, joy, peace, patience, kindness, goodness, faithfulness, gentleness, and self-control.

A life filled with the Spirit is a life filled with these attributes of God.

This is the litmus test for the condition of your walk with God. Paul tells us these are the results of a life led by the Holy Spirit. Take some time to evaluate your life.

Does your life exude these fruits?

You may say, "Well, those are difficult qualities to maintain." You would be right, *if* you're trying to do it on your own! You can't achieve these at a divine, Spirit-filled level without embracing the Spirit that fills you. The Blueprint is clear – If you embrace the lifechanging truth that you are the temple of the Holy Spirit, you can achieve this kind of fruit in your life. The more the Holy Spirit is in the forefront of your life, the more these qualities are naturally manifested. You are a tree designed to bear fruit.

God desires that you grow and thrive. You can always improve. You can always stop settling for less. If you're not progressing, you're regressing.

There is a supernatural force that dwells within you as a believer. He will lead you into a deeper understanding of His Word. He will give you confidence to be the light He's called you to be. He will breathe through you truth that can change the lives of those around you.

The Holy Spirit is capable of doing more than you ever dreamed possible. As your life produces fruit, that fruit will be a testimony of the saving power of the Gospel.

All you need to do is believe it, and live it, walking by the power of the Holy Spirit.

Thoughts from Chapter 4: Filled

When you became a believer in Jesus Christ, you were filled with the Holy Spirit. You don't have to worry about not having enough of the Spirit. God filled you to the brim with an ever-flowing abundance of His Spirit. The Holy Spirit is literally the presence of Jesus Christ in your life, helping you understand and apply His Word, pray, receive wisdom, and experience spiritual fruit including love, joy, and peace. Many Christians struggle because they try to live by their own design instead of walking by the Spirit. You must decrease so He can increase in your life. The more you surrender to the Spirit's leading, the more you'll experience His infinite power. The Comforter was given so you could be a conqueror.

Questions to Consider

What does it mean to be Spirit-filled?

Have you ever felt like you had a deficiency of the Holy Spirit? Why?

Have you ever struggled to understand God's Word or know what to pray? How can you better align yourself with the Holy Spirit to experience His help and direction?

Describe a specific time when the Holy Spirit spoke to you and guided you. What was that like?

In what areas of your life do you need to decrease so the Holy Spirit can increase?

Additional Verses to Study / How Can i Apply This?

- Luke 11:9-13

- Ephesians 1:12-23

- 1 Thessalonians 1:4-7

- Isaiah 11:1-5

- Luke 4:14-21

Building Blocks: Before i Move On...

☐ I am Spirit-filled.

☐ I am communicating with Christ daily through the Holy Spirit. He is teaching me to understand His Word and helping me to pray boldly.

☐ I am seeking the Holy Spirit's direction in my daily life. As I make decisions each day, I want more of Him and less of me.

☐ I am experiencing the fruit of the Spirit including love, joy, and peace. I am actively sharing these fruits with others.

Prayer

Heavenly Father, I confess that I am not able to understand and apply Your Word by my own ability. I need Your help! I praise You for the gift of the Holy Spirit. I thank You for filling me with Your Spirit to lead me into all truth and empower me to do Your will. I hunger for more of the Holy Spirit's direction in my daily life. Help me to seek Your will in every decision and be attentive to Your voice, remaining obedient to Your spoken and written Word. Help me to experience a sanctified life, full of the fruit of the Spirit, and actively sharing that fruit with others. Amen.

CHAPTER 5
SHOWERS

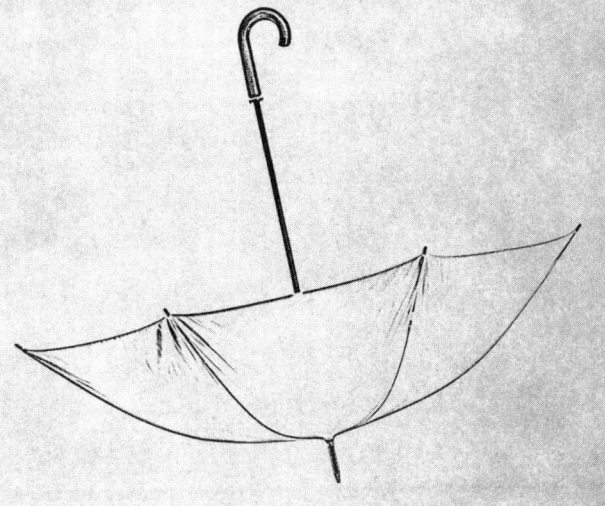

For everything there is a season, a time for every activity under heaven. A time to be born and a time to die. A time to plant and a time to harvest. A time to kill and a time to heal. A time to tear down and a time to build up. A time to cry and a time to laugh. A time to grieve and a time to dance. A time to scatter stones and a time to gather stones. A time to embrace and a time to turn away. A time to search and a time to quit searching. A time to keep and a time to throw away. A time to tear and a time to mend. A time to be quiet and a time to speak. A time to love and a time to hate. A time for war and a time for peace.

Ecclesiastes 3:1-8

I struggle with the ups and downs of life. Do you? Sometimes I feel like a pogo stick on steroids. When life is good, I wonder how long it will last. When things are bad, I wonder if I can make it through. It can be an exhausting cycle.

Over the years I've learned some valuable lessons regarding God's Blueprint for the seasons of life. I certainly haven't achieved perfection, but by God's grace I've come to better understand the seasons I face, enjoy, and labor through. Seasons come and seasons go. Some seasons last for years and others last for days. Seasons are like us – temporary, like the morning fog.

How do you know what your life will be like tomorrow? Your life is like the morning fog—it's here a little while, then it's gone.

James 4:14

What season are you in?

Is your life filled with heartache? Are you wounded and grieving? Are you basking in accomplishment and success? Are you rejoicing in new blessings?

The grand Architect who keeps all things in motion – the Unmoved Mover – is unchanged in any season. Your Father in Heaven has a perfect understanding of every season you go through. The seasons of your life are earthly canvases that allow you to experience the brush strokes of a loving God rich in grace and mercy.

Both days of victory and nights of tears are in the hands of the Potter who can bring us peace in every season.

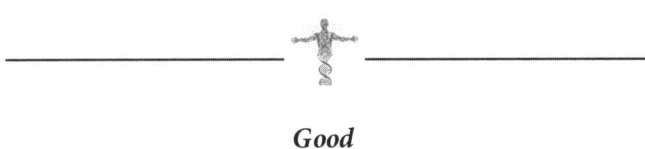

Good

One of the most encouraging yet misunderstood verses in the Bible is Romans 8:28,

> *And we know that God causes everything to work together for the good of those who love God and are called according to his purpose for them.*

I've often heard this verse quoted in a way that offers nothing more than a false sense of security to a person in distress. This is not a promise given to all people who attend church on Sunday. This isn't a superficial truth for anyone who believes in a "higher power" or has a cross around their neck. This is not a feel-good verse we can share with someone who needs encouragement as we rush through a conversation in passing.

This is a declaration of truth powerful enough to shake the world.

Romans 8:28 will either invigorate you with hope and confidence *or* point you to the very source of why your ups and downs are more about the downs than the ups.

Let's take a deeper look into what this promise actually says.

And we know: Paul knew a thing or two about ups and downs in life. When the Holy Spirit breathed these words through Paul, I have to believe that Paul's eyes were welling with tears. One day Paul was in jail and the next he witnessed miracles. One day Paul was beaten with lashes and the next he saw the church thrive as God anointed his work and poured out His blessings. Paul knew firsthand the uncertainty of life, yet the verse confidently reads, "And we know…"

Your faith is the staple of every season.

What is faith? Hebrews 11:1 declares:

> *Faith is the confidence that what we hope for will actually happen; it gives us assurance about things we cannot see.*

Where are you in your walk with Jesus Christ, the Lover and Redeemer of your soul? Do you believe that the One who conquered the grave can also master your seasons?

God causes: In every season of life – good or bad – God is ultimately in control. We are not God and we are not in control as much as we think we are. God spoke a word and there were oceans. God spoke a word and time began. God's purpose is greater than His people. God is the Author, the Foundation, the First Cause of everything that exists. He causes…

…everything to work together: Everything is not "most things." Everything is literally every thing. Almost every time I hear Romans 8:28 quoted, it's during a time of struggle or hardship. But if we are going to claim this verse on the "downs" we must also claim it on the "ups." This passage is just as much about God's purpose as it is about His provision. God desires every aspect of our lives to be focused around His good. *Everything.* That's every promotion as well as every layoff. Every healthy doctor's visit *and* every poor bill of health. In both our triumphant days and in the days we pray would end – God causes *everything* to work together…

…for the good: This is not a promise that God is going to take away your cancer and give you a Corvette, though He could. But there is a massive difference between our "good" and God's "good." God breathed the universe into existence and declared it to be "good." We eat a cheese pizza and say "it's good." There is no comparison between the trivial way we use the word "good," and the way God uses the word "good." Our "good" is based on the limited bit of knowledge we get through our five senses. But God's "good" is rooted in *infinite understanding* and *eternal purpose.* God works everything together for *His good*, and not necessarily what we think is "good." God's "good" is what's godly for us and what brings Him glory. Sometimes God gives us the things we want in order to bring glory to Himself. But sometimes, God withholds the things we want in order to glorify Himself by producing in us a godliness and goodness beyond our limited understanding. We need to acknowledge that God's way of doing things is better than our way, in both the good times and the bad. We can't pray Romans 8:28 in times of hardship and then walk away from it in times of excess. If your heart and mind aren't passionate about "good" equaling "glory to God no matter what," Romans 8:28 will simply not grip you with peace and purpose.

of those who love God: When I went to close on my first house, the stack of paperwork was astounding. I was only interested in one thing – the final price. The top page listed all the important information that I needed to know to become a homeowner. Very few people read all the fine print – most just skim through it or skip over it. There is never any fine print in God's Word. Every word of Scripture is "large print" intended to be read carefully, not skipped over.

That's why this phrase "of those who love God" is so important. The God who knows our desires and promises abundance is causing everything to work together for good – *for those who love Him.*

Do you love God? Are you passionately in love with Him? In John 14:15, Jesus says, *"If you love me, obey my commandments."*

Our love for God is reflected in our willingness to keep His commandments. God's commandments are the rebar of His Blueprint. In order for us to achieve the work God desires of us, we must be willing to keep His commandments. Jesus didn't die so we could continue sinning. He died so we would not only be forgiven of our sin, but experience victory over it!

By the power of Christ dwelling in us through the Holy Spirit, we are called to love God with all our heart, soul, mind, and strength (Luke 10:27). Your love for God should cause you to search your heart, root out known sin, and eliminate it from your life. Jesus gave His life to save you from disobedience; this is why He said, "If you love me you will do your very best to remain in obedience" (my paraphrase). The reality is that we all sin. But are you living a life of holiness with occasional failure, or are you living a life of failure with occasional holiness? As believers, our lives should be characterized by righteousness, not sin. We should be pursuing a lifestyle of continual godliness. The more we obey God's Word, the more we can fully experience a life engulfed in love. His Word is sweet and wholesome. Like a love letter to you, His instruction leads to a sure confidence in every season.

called according to his purpose for them: Jeremiah 29:11 says it best,

> *"For I know the plans I have for you," says the LORD. "They are plans for good and not for disaster, to give you a future and a hope."*

God's way is the best way. Time and time again you find the word "good" in passages regarding His will for your life. God has good things for you – *infinitely good things!*

On the next page, write down your current life situation – your family, church, job, studies, health, finances, possessions, plans, goals, and dreams. Slowly go through each area of your life, calculating what percentage of each revolves around your purpose and what percentage revolves around God's purpose.

Did you do it? If you didn't, put the book down and stop reading. The rest won't matter. If we can't learn to successfully navigate the seasons of life, it's only a matter of time before we throw in the towel. Better to throw it in now, experience humbling defeat, and then rebuild on the principles of Romans 8:28 with His purpose anchoring the fiber of your faith. Sometimes we learn the hard way, but we don't have to.

The passage that piloted me through the roughest seasons of my life is Proverbs 3:5-7, which declares:

> *Trust in the LORD with all your heart; do not depend on your own understanding. Seek his will in all you do, and he will show you which path to take. Don't be impressed with your own wisdom. Instead, fear the LORD and turn away from evil.*

My Purpose	His Purpose

No matter what the season, God's good is better than our understanding. The promise of Romans 8:28 assures that with God's help we can successfully navigate whatever lies ahead.

Umbrellas

I will send you the seasonal rains. The land will then yield its crops, and the trees of the field will produce their fruit.

Leviticus 26:4

If you ask most children what they think of rain, odds are they'll smile and tell you they love jumping in puddles. If you ask most farmers what they think of rain, they'd probably tell you it depends on how much and how often they get it. If you asked my grandfather what he thought about rain, he'd tell you he finds it depressing.

On a hot day, rain can feel refreshing to the body. On a cold day, with the wind blowing, rain can be miserable and uncomfortable. Rain is a mesmerizing phenomenon to begin with. One moment the sun is shining, then clouds slowly roll in and it isn't long before drops of water pour out from the heavens by the quintillions. Have you ever been caught in a powerful downpour?

Every once in awhile we'll get a bad storm at our house right when we need to leave for an outing. For some reason, umbrellas are always there when you don't need them, but the moment you need one they all seem to disappear. After scrambling around the house searching for an umbrella and not being able to find one, we decide to tough it out with a mad dash to the car in the pouring rain. Before we make our run for it we decide who is opening what doors, on which sides, at what times – a strategic plan for optimum dryness. I always think to myself during those take-a-picture moments, "As fun as this is, it sure would be nice to have an umbrella!"

Do you ever lose yourself in the simple day-to-day wonders of life? For me, there are not many things more relaxing than standing in the rain with an umbrella. Rain is coming down all around you, and yet, in your little three-foot space is a calmness enabling you to safely experience the storm.

God's promises are an umbrella for the storms of life. We can use God's umbrella of promise to navigate four seasons of showers we encounter: trials, tribulations, resting, and blessings. Two of these seasons are our "ups" and two are our "downs."

Which are you in now?

Holding the Umbrella Right-Side Up

Dear brothers and sisters, when troubles come your way, consider it an opportunity for great joy. For you know that when your faith is tested, your endurance has a chance to grow. So let it grow, for when your endurance is fully developed, you will be perfect and complete, needing nothing.

James 1:2-4

Nobody is excited about going through tough times. I've never heard one person say, "I love the down seasons in life!" This passage from the book of James is challenging. Every time I read, "an opportunity," I am greatly convicted. The honest reality is, I dread going through tough times. My shoulders grow weak by the weight of the pressure and stress. Can you relate? I never liked taking tests in school, and tests in real life are even worse. Building endurance in the gym is tough, and building endurance in our faith is even tougher.

However, I love the latter part of this passage, "you will be perfect and complete, needing nothing." I don't know about you, but I want that! In times of testing, there is a purpose. There is a method to the madness. The Architect knows exactly what I need in order to accomplish a great work in me.

God's love for us is so great that He allows us to go through situations that break His heart in order to break us for His heart. This is divine devastation.

When we struggle in life, we're either going through a trial or a tribulation. Many people think these words mean the same thing. Although the symptoms may be similar, trials and tribulations are actually vastly different.

A trial is a season of challenge that God allows us to go through in order to test and grow our faith. A tribulation, on the other hand, is a season of hardship caused by sin – whether that be our own sins or the sins of those around us. Trials are orchestrated by our Heavenly Father to build our faith. Tribulations are the work of Satan to destroy our faith. But the umbrella of God's promises remains our steadfast protection in either season.

Recognizing a Trial: There is perhaps no greater trial than the one experienced by Joseph in the Old Testament (Genesis 37-50). Joseph was the eleventh of twelve sons born to Jacob. Jacob deeply loved Joseph. Joseph's life, in his early years, was seemingly wonderful. He loved God and was devoted to caring for his father's flocks. The Bible tells us in Genesis 37 that Joseph was his father's favorite son. Jacob even gave Joseph a beautiful robe of many colors to show his affection for him. Joseph was blessed by God, even at a young age. This created great jealousy in the hearts of his brothers, who plotted to take Joseph's life. Joseph was ripped away from his father, thrown in a pit, sold into slavery, falsely accused of a crime, and imprisoned for two years – all while being separated from his family and homeland. This was a true time of testing and challenge, yet nowhere do we read that Joseph ever doubted God or gave up. As we read through Joseph's story we discover an important truth when it comes to recognizing a trial. Genesis 39:2 reads:

> *The LORD was with Joseph, so he succeeded in everything he did as he served in the home of his Egyptian master.*

Over and over you will find the words, "The LORD was with Joseph." God wants us to know that in the middle of all Joseph was going through, He was with him. Joseph was never alone. Joseph was never left to fend for himself. God was with Joseph.

Is God with you? How do you know? As I've read this story through the years, I often asked myself how Joseph knew that God was with him. How did Joseph remain so faithful and unwavering?

In order to know when we're going through a trial, we must know God is with us. The only way we can know that God is with us is to spend time with Him. If we are passionately walking with God, we're going to know beyond a shadow of a doubt that He's there. Joseph was tempted and yet he remained faithful. He was pressed, yet remained devoted. He knew God daily and denounced sin as it was presented. He was walking with God and knew God was with him.

If you are going through a time of testing, ask yourself, "Is God with me?" If you feel distant from Him, seek His presence. Joseph's story ends with an incredible downpour of God's blessings on his life. Joseph stayed faithful in the tough times, and God blessed him in the good times. Not only was Joseph freed from prison, but he also became second-in-command over the entire land of Egypt. God then warned him of a coming famine and used him to save millions of people from starvation. The story ends with Joseph forgiving his brothers, being reconciled with them, and being reunited with his father Jacob. God took something as awful as being sold into slavery, and in a way that only God could, turned it around into something glorious.

It's a powerful story of trials and triumph. A trial produces perfection and completeness. God allows us to go through trials because it draws us closer to Him while teaching us endurance.

Just imagine if Joseph had never gone through these trials. He would have never gone to Egypt, he would not have warned anyone of the coming famine, and countless people would have starved. Not only that, but Joseph's relationship with his brothers would not have been repaired, and his own spiritual growth would have stagnated. As painful as the trials were, they were necessary for God's perfect will to ultimately be accomplished.

If we are faithful and obedient to God, we can confidently tackle a trial because we know our lives are in tune with God's will. No matter how bad things were, Joseph trusted that God had a plan. He knew he wasn't being punished or abandoned by his Heavenly Father. God was present with him each step of the way, and God ultimately brought him safely through the trials and into a season of great blessings.

Trials are perfecting.

Recognizing a Tribulation: I have faced more tribulations in my life than trials. Some tribulations are brought on by the sins of others. Some come by our own sins. Either way, tribulations are sin-driven.

Perhaps this is why James writes,

> *And remember, when you are being tempted, do not say, "God is tempting me." God is never tempted to do wrong, and he never tempts anyone else. Temptation comes from our own desires, which entice us and drag us away. These desires give birth to sinful actions. And when sin is allowed to grow, it gives birth to death.*
>
> *James 1:13-15*

As I recall that storefront where I was broken and weeping, I now realize I was experiencing tribulation. God was not tempting me. My own selfish desires and disobedience led me to that place.

Tribulations are terrifying.

Although God can forgive our sins, the natural consequences of sin don't disappear. God is faithful in His pursuit of your perfection. Good parents who love their children discipline them. How many times have you been told, "Don't touch that, it's hot!" I've said that hundreds of times to my children. But when do we *really* find out how hot it is? When we touch it! Sometimes God's greatest form of discipline is simply allowing us to experience the scrapes and bruises from our own falls. He allows us to experience the inevitable results of our own decisions. *That's how we learn.* Hebrews 12:5-6 encourages us with this:

> *And have you forgotten the encouraging words God spoke to you as his children? He said, "My child, don't make light of the LORD's discipline, and don't give up when he corrects you. For the LORD disciplines those he loves, and he punishes each one he accepts as his child."*

God's umbrella provides divine clarity in the middle of life's storms. We often cannot understand why we're going through a certain situation. But God understands, and He is faithful in convicting us of sin that causes tribulation. God gives us wisdom and direction in understanding the root causes.

Are you:

- Financially destitute?
- In an unstable marriage?
- On the verge of a breakdown?
- Plotting revenge?
- Feeling worthless?

Ask yourself this question: *Why?*

Take some time to revel in the clarity that comes from being under God's umbrella. Take a moment to consider Hebrews 12:12-13, which says:

> *So take a new grip with your tired hands and strengthen your weak knees. Mark out a straight path for your feet so that those who are weak and lame will not fall but become strong.*

When we are facing a tribulation we must take a steadfast look at what our lives have become, and search our hearts for God's direction. Prideful financial decisions, selfish relationships, poor priorities, lack of forgiveness and love, focusing on materialism and surface beauty – these are the kinds of problems God reveals to us in times of tribulation. Those who trust God in tribulation are able to praise Him in the midst of it, instead of blaming Him for it. He is faithful in revealing the error of our ways. As He reveals the roots of our pain, we can greatly rejoice, because once we understand the cause of a problem, we can learn how to fix it.

Tribulations are purifying.

If others are attacking you because of your faith, take heart in knowing God is with you. 2 Timothy 3:12 tells us *"everyone who wants to live a godly life in Christ Jesus will suffer persecution."* Persecution is not an "if" but a "when." How you handle those times of challenge is what defines your testimony to a lost world.

> *God blesses those who are persecuted for doing right, for the Kingdom of Heaven is theirs. God blesses you when people mock you and persecute you and lie about you and say all sorts of evil things against you because you are my followers. Be happy about it! Be very glad! For a great reward awaits you in heaven. And remember, the ancient prophets were persecuted in the same way.*
>
> Matthew 5:10-12

In the midst of persecution are God's blessings. Instead of repaying evil for evil, choose to love, forgive, and remain under God's umbrella of mercy. Be prayerful for the right words to say. Be humble with a heart to serve. If you can avoid persecution, do so. But if not, embrace it. At one point or another we all face persecution beyond our control. Our response should be joy, for by not allowing the persecution to defeat us, we bring God glory.

Tribulations are magnifying.

Resting: Even as we go through trials and tribulations, God offers us a pavilion of rest and wisdom. We can rest in knowing that God is rich in mercy. Your Creator understands your limitations and weaknesses. When we find ourselves in the midst of a storm, it's easy to doubt God's provision. But even when we don't have the strength to hold on, His umbrella shields us. God's pavilion does not require our strength to sustain it. It simply requires our willingness to remain under it.

> *God is our refuge and strength, always ready to help in times of trouble.*
>
> Psalm 46:1

"God is." It's not about you! God's awesome refuge is all about Him. He protects us not just for our own benefit, but to bring glory to Himself. Trials are a time for us to trust that God is doing a great work that will ultimately bring Him glory while building us up in the process. An old saying goes, "When you're down to nothing, God is up to something." Although the ground may shake, the mountains may crumble, and the oceans may roar – God is still in control. Rest under His umbrella. Let go of the handle and rest. Let the God who is creating endurance in your faith replenish your spirit with the strength to finish what was started.

Flipping the Umbrella Upside Down

What do people really get for all their hard work? I have seen the burden God has placed on us all. Yet God has made everything beautiful for its own time. He has planted eternity in the human heart, but even so, people cannot see the whole scope of God's work from beginning to end. So I concluded there is nothing better than to be happy and enjoy ourselves as long as we can. And people should eat and drink and enjoy the fruits of their labor, for these are gifts from God. And I know that whatever God does is final. Nothing can be added to it or taken from it. God's purpose is that people should fear him.

Ecclesiastes 3:9-14

Do you bail before the blessings? Although God gives us an umbrella that provides refuge in times of trials, revelation in the time of tribulation, and resting in the time of weakness, we were never meant to stay there indefinitely. In fact, I believe that God desires us to live our lives with His umbrella upside down more than live with it right-side up.

Francis Chan – one of the great authors and pastors of our day – said, "The more we deceive ourselves, the more content we become."

God provides shelter from the storms of life, but those storms last only a season. Once the storm is over, God asks us to step out from the shelter and accomplish His work in the world. Being a Christian is so much more than just weathering a storm, and resting for a brief moment before the next storm hits. Although trials and tribulations will come, our lives should not be defined by them. What God ultimately desires for our lives is blessings. Jesus came so we can experience a life that is "full and complete" (Ephesians 1:23) and "rich and satisfying" (John 10:10).

Life is not about surviving. It's about thriving!

Students take tests so they can earn a degree. Who would pass all the tests, but not show up to graduation? The purpose of the tests is to get you to the graduation. *The same is true in life.*

Often, we get so close to the end of an intense trial, but then we give up. We get within days – maybe even hours – of accomplishing a great work, and then we quit. *We bail before the blessings!*

Farmers plant seeds and work the fields, expecting to reap a bountiful harvest. They labor and sweat in the hot sun because they need the harvest. They embrace the rain because it benefits the crops. There has never been a farmer in the history of agriculture who walked away from the crops a day before the harvest. Jesus is no different. He says:

> *I am the true grapevine, and my Father is the gardener. He cuts off every branch of mine that doesn't produce fruit, and he prunes the branches that do bear fruit so they will produce even more. You have already been pruned and purified by the message I have given you. Remain in me, and I will remain in you. For a branch cannot produce fruit if it is severed from the vine, and you cannot be fruitful unless you remain in me. Yes, I am the vine; you are the branches. Those who remain in me, and I in them, will produce much fruit. For apart from me you can do nothing. Anyone who does not remain in me is thrown away like a useless branch and withers. Such branches are gathered into a pile to be burned. But if you remain in me and my words remain in you, you may ask for anything you want, and it will be granted! When you produce much fruit, you are my true disciples. This brings great glory to my Father. I have loved you even as the Father has loved me. Remain in my love. When you obey my commandments, you remain in my love, just as I obey my Father's commandments and remain in his love. I have told you these things so that you will be filled with my joy. Yes, your joy will overflow!*
>
> *John 15:1-11*

The Blueprint for every season of your life is: *Remain in Christ.*

Wherever He is leading you is where you need to be. If He's leading you through a trial, patiently endure it. If you're in a tribulation, eliminate the sin that caused it. Whatever the season, remain in Him. The more we remain in Him, the more endurance we build in our faith and the more blessings we ultimately receive. We take the umbrella that shields us from the storms and we flip it upside down to catch God's blessings.

John 15:1-11 is a promise for the determined. We must remain:

- In His Word (2 Timothy 2:15).
- In prayer (1 Thessalonians 5:17).
- Confident of His promises (Hebrews 3:6).
- Faithful (John 8:31, 1 John 2:24).
- Obedient (John 15:10, 1 John 3:24).
- In His love (John 15:9).

God's Blueprint is His authoritative declaration of how life works. Although everything else in the universe continually changes, *the Blueprint never changes.* If we remain in Christ, we will experience an abundant and satisfying life. Are you passionate about remaining?

> *So do not throw away this confident trust in the Lord. Remember the great reward it brings you! Patient endurance is what you need now, so that you will continue to do God's will. Then you will receive all that he has promised.*
>
> Hebrews 10:35-36

Thoughts from Chapter 5: Showers

Life is literally made of seasons. Some seasons are "ups" and some are "downs." Your ability to navigate through the "down" seasons of life determines your ability to enjoy more "up" seasons than "down" seasons. Trials are times of testing that ultimately perfect you. Tribulations are times of suffering caused by sin. The umbrella of God's promise in Romans 8:28 offers you clarity and wisdom to navigate every season. You can rest knowing that God's umbrella protects you in difficult seasons. But God also calls you to step out from under the umbrella and flip it upside down to catch His blessings. God desires you to live a life that is full, complete, abundant, and satisfying. Don't bail before the blessings!

Questions to Consider

Do you experience more "down" seasons than "up" seasons in your life? Why?

What have you learned from Romans 8:28?

What is the difference between a trial and a tribulation? Are you going through one of these now? How do you know?

Do you get mad at God in times of tribulation?

What are some steps you can take to activate a faith that experiences showers of blessings more frequently?

Additional Verses to Study / How Can i Apply This?

- Ezekiel 34:25-31

- Psalm 27

- Psalm 94:12-14

- Psalm 139:23-24

- Job 1 and Job 42

Building Blocks: Before i Move On...

☐ I believe that God is in control of every season.

☐ I am living in obedience to God's Word, knowing that "God causes everything to work together for the good of those who love God and are called according to his purpose for them." (Romans 8:28)

☐ I am prayerfully seeking clarity to better understand the season I'm currently in. If it is a trial, I am committed to patiently enduring it. If it is a tribulation, I am committed to removing the sin that caused it.

☐ I will not bail before the blessings. I believe God desires me to experience an abundance of "up" seasons in my life.

Prayer

Heavenly Father, I praise You for the promise of Romans 8:28. Please give me clarity to understand every season. Give me patience to endure every trial without bailing before the blessings. Give me strength to remove from my life every sin that causes tribulation. Please help me to remain confident of Your promises and obedient to Your Word so I will fully experience the full and complete life You designed me for. Amen.

CHAPTER 6
JARS

Commit your actions to the LORD, and your plans will succeed.

Proverbs 16:3

Time. Talents. Finances. Relationships. These four areas of life often consume our focus. How we approach them will either define our faith or defile it. They are battlegrounds for God's glory or the world's gluttony.

We are called to be good stewards of what God blesses us with by His grace. Grace is the free and unmerited favor of God, as manifested in the salvation of sinners and the bestowal of blessings.

The beauty of God's grace is that He is unlimited in His inventory and is able to fill you with blessings beyond overflowing. Remember, God is the Potter and you are the clay. As He shapes you into the vessel He desires you to be, and as you remain faithful to Him in the process, He will entrust you with His blessings. But with blessings come responsibility. In the Parable of the Unjust Steward (Luke 16:10-11), Jesus said:

> *"If you are faithful in little things, you will be faithful in large ones. But if you are dishonest in little things, you won't be honest with greater responsibilities. And if you are untrustworthy about worldly wealth, who will trust you with the true riches of heaven?"*

God is eager to pour out His blessings on those who obediently manage them for His glory. I realize that some would say, "That makes no sense. What about non-believers with plenty of wealth who seem to have an abundance even if they aren't managing it obediently?"

God isn't nearly as concerned about material possessions as we are. The wealth of this world will soon pass away. But the blessings we receive and the way we steward them have eternal value. And while the Bible is clear that all good and perfect gifts are from God (James 1:17), we are more than mere recipients of good gifts. We are ambassadors of the Kingdom of God (2 Corinthians 5:20). We are royalty, called to reflect the awesome unmerited grace of our Heavenly Father. While others may be playing life by a different set of rules, we've been bathed in grace and changed forever. This grace is now flowing in our lives like a refreshing stream of cool water. *Share it!*

How is your stewardship? When you make out your calendar for the month, is God at the forefront of each event scheduled? Are your talents and skills being utilized for God's glory? Does the way you handle your finances reflect a generous love for others? Do your relationships with others reflect your relationship with Christ? This is where the rubber meets the road.

This Is All I Have

*One day the widow of a member of the group of prophets came to Elisha and cried out, "My husband who served you is dead, and you know how he feared the LORD. But now a creditor has come, threatening to take my two sons as slaves." "What can I do to help you?" Elisha asked. "Tell me, what do you have in the house?" "Nothing at all, **except** a flask of olive oil," she replied. And Elisha said, "**Borrow** as many empty jars as you can from your friends and neighbors. Then go into your house with your sons and **shut the door** behind you. Pour olive oil from your flask into the jars, setting each one aside when it is filled." So she did as she was told. Her sons kept bringing jars to her, and she filled one after another. Soon **every container was full** to the brim! "Bring me another jar," she said to one of her sons. "**There aren't any more!**" he told her. And then the olive oil stopped flowing.*

2 Kings 4:1-6

There is much we can learn from this passage of Scripture about God's blessings and how to live a FAVORful life.

It's not about how much, but about how willing: When the prophet Elisha asked the woman what she had, she responded, "Nothing at all, except...." What matters isn't the amount of blessings you have, but your willingness to surrender them for God's purpose. This widow was down to just a little oil in one flask. Her home was on the line. Her children were on the line. She had nothing, "except...."

What you have is borrowed: Elisha tells the widow to go and borrow as many jars as she can. She had to borrow them because she had no money to buy them. She was bankrupt. We once owed a debt so great there was nothing we could do to repay it, but Jesus Christ paid that debt in full. We are bankrupt without Him. Ultimately, everything we have is borrowed from God. He is the maker and provider of all things. We may work, but He gives us the strength to work. We may create, but He gives us the ability to create. We may be gifted in talents, organization, leadership, compassion, business, or relationships, but He is the source of all these gifts. Stewardship means not only receiving blessings, but also using them to be one who blesses. Everything we have – all our possessions and abilities – belong to God. Since everything we have is borrowed from Him, we must use everything we have for Him.

Everything should point to Jesus: My favorite part of this passage is, "shut the door." If God was going to work a miracle for this widow, it would have to be done by Him and Him alone. The widow took the borrowed jars and shut the door. There was no interference. There was no outside influence. There was no one else present who could possibly take credit for the miracle about to happen, and there was no other possible explanation for it except divine intervention. God and God alone would receive the glory. Does God receive the glory for the blessings in your life? The devil tries hard to get us to take credit for our successes. But when we start believing that we created our own blessings, we take ownership instead of borrowship. As soon as we think we're "entitled" to something, we forget that everything we have is a gift from God, freely given out of His infinite love and unmerited grace. As soon as we take credit for the gifts God gives us, we rob God of the glory He deserves. If the widow had refused to shut the door, no miracle would have happened.

The more jars you have, the more blessings you receive: The jars were collected, the tops were off, and they were waiting to be filled. Each area of our lives that we deny God control over is like a jar sealed tight, closed to God's abundance.

- If you have a tight grip on your finances, God can't bless them.
- If your marriage is controlled by your own stubborn pride or lust, God can't bless it.
- If you schedule your time according to your own desires instead of God's will for your life, He can't bless it.

God can't bless what He doesn't have access to. You must remove the lid and let Him have control.

As the jars were filled, they were filled to the brim. God knows exactly what will fill you. He knows what will complete you. He will waste nothing and use everything in a way that will bring you peace and purpose. By design, only He can fill you to the brim.

Fear begins where your faith ends: The only reason the oil stopped flowing is because there were no more jars to fill. How many jars would you have collected if you were her sons? One? Two? Ten?

In other words, how great is your faith? Would you have taken the time to collect 100 jars, believing that they would *all* be filled?

What keeps us from surrendering everything to God? Usually, it's because we don't really believe that He can manage our time, talents, finances, and relationships better than we can. We trust in our own abilities more than we trust in God. We don't surrender everything to Him because we're *afraid* of what would happen if we did.

Fear is the opposite of faith.

Faith says God can.

Fear says you can.

Maybe you're a new believer, and the thought of fully surrendering your time, talents, finances, and relationships to God scares you. Maybe you feel like you have so little to offer that it doesn't even matter. Or perhaps you feel like you have too much to give up. Whatever jars you have, God is more qualified to work perfection and purpose in them than you are.

What defines your life – faith or fear?

The Fear of Faith

Fear is powerful. At one time, the fear of failure gripped my life. The fear of the unknown suffocated the peace from me. The fear of inadequacy crippled me. Fear can ruin our lives and change who we are, but only if we allow it to.

> *For God has not given us a spirit of fear and timidity, but of power, love, and self-discipline.*
>
> *2 Timothy 1:7*

God is not the author of fear, but the giver of power, love, and self-discipline. Yet in a perplexing dynamic, the Bible tells us that our faith in God should produce a fear of Him.

> *Fear of the LORD leads to life, bringing security and protection from harm.*
>
> *Proverbs 19:23*

How can the Bible declare that God is not the author of fear, yet command us to fear Him? I've heard few teachings on what it means to fear the LORD. Most focus on His wrath, doing this truth an injustice.

> *Such love has no fear, because perfect love expels all fear. If we are afraid, it is for fear of punishment, and this shows that we have not fully experienced his perfect love.*
>
> *1 John 4:18*

Our perception of the word "fear" is based on punishment and pain. But God's design for us is love. In His love, we can rest in the truth that He is for us and not against us. God desires to bring us blessings and abundance.

Fearing God means understanding the sorrow that comes from being separated from Him. It means coming face to face with the uncertainty of life without Him. It's that awesome moment when we realize that the AUTHOR has full AUTHORity. By design, God declares that we do not need to fear life's circumstances. What we *do* need to fear is a life separated from His will.

Do you fear God enough to have every jar of your life open and surrendered before Him? The God of the universe is letting you borrow His infinite blessings. He is trusting you with His greatest gifts and asking you to honor Him with them.

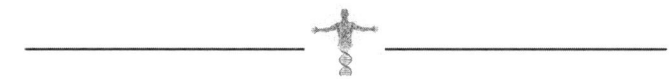

Time

> *But you must not forget this one thing, dear friends: A day is like a thousand years to the Lord, and a thousand years is like a day.*
>
> *2 Peter 3:8*

The world is a hectic place of on-the-go agendas and plans. Most of us are so busy we've forgotten why we're so busy in the first place! 2 Peter 3:8 is an awesome reminder of why we need to pause to consider God's will when it comes to our time. Although we may feel like we don't have enough time to accomplish God's will for our lives, the reality is that God has given us everything we need. A single day can accomplish a thousand years worth of work if God is involved. Nothing is impossible for Him.

Rest for a moment in that.

God is beyond time. He's not restrained by clocks or pressured by deadlines. Why do we feel the weight of the calendar, experience the anxiety of the alarm, or stress over years gone by? Because we don't fully surrender our time to God. Instead of allowing the Holy Spirit to lead and guide us moment by moment, we would rather stick to our own schedules. We think we can manage our time better than God can.

But consider this: God existed from eternity past, and He understands what the future holds far better than you do. His plan for you is perfect. But it can't be accomplished until you surrender your time to God.

> *Unfailing love and faithfulness make atonement for sin. By fearing the LORD, people avoid evil. When people's lives please the LORD, even their enemies are at peace with them. Better to have little, with godliness, than to be rich and dishonest. We can make our plans, but the LORD determines our steps.*
>
> *Proverbs 16:6-9*

The reality is, we often make plans without a fear of the LORD in our hearts. The original Hebrew word for "make our plans" is *chashab*, meaning "to plot" or "to fabricate." This word is rooted in malicious intent. We probably don't intend for our busyness to be malicious. In fact, we usually think we are busy doing *good* things!

But God doesn't want good. He wants *best*. We can spend every moment doing good deeds, but if our actions are purely our own plans and not God's will, we've failed to live our lives to the fullest. The life *best* lived is a life fully surrendered to God's will. In order for God's will to be accomplished in our lives, we need to spend less time pursuing our own ambitions and desires, and more time obediently following His direction according to His Word and the inspiration of the Holy Spirit.

Are you working so hard to earn money that you rarely spend quality time with your family, or in God's Word? Do you spend so much time exercising and trying to get the perfect body that you neglect your relationships with others and with God? Are you a parent overwhelmed with a multitude of programs and sports for your kids? Are you constantly struggling, caught in the endless pursuit of "happiness"?

It amazes me how busy we get trying to juggle the demands of work, school, family, friends, health, and our spiritual lives. Life quickly spirals out of control whenever we try to manage these things ourselves instead of giving them to God. Although we do many things with good intentions, our plans are often driven by our own self-centeredness and need for control. We want to make our own schedules. We think we know what we need to be happy. And even worse, we think we know what others need to be happy.

Do your kids really don't need you to work overtime so you can afford a bigger house, nicer car, or that $200 pair of Nike's they want?

What they need is for you to demonstrate biblical leadership and invest *time* in them.

It's great to exercise to improve your health and appearance, but don't strive for artificial Hollywoodism. Be a treasure, not a trophy.

Don't get so caught up in programs and activities that you forget to enjoy the simple things of life with those you love.

Stop pursuing happiness by your own strength, and start enjoying God's free gift of joy through His grace.

Happiness is temporary. The more we pursue it, the more time it demands. It's constantly changing. Happiness is slippery. We struggle and struggle to grab hold of it, and as soon as we do, it slips right through our fingers. But joy means letting go. It means surrendering everything to God, taking a deep breath, and simply basking in the peace that comes from trusting Him. Joy is so much greater than happiness. Dr. James MacDonald once said, "Joy makes happy look stupid."

Joy comes from having a full jar. God fills the jar when we fully surrender to Him.

> *God has now revealed to us his mysterious plan regarding Christ, a plan to fulfill his own good pleasure. And this is the plan:* **At the right time** *he will bring everything together under the authority of Christ—everything in heaven and on earth. Furthermore, because we are united with Christ, we have received an inheritance from God, for he chose us in advance, and he makes everything work out according to his plan.*
>
> Ephesians 1:9-11

Is your time God's time? Are you busy going about your own business, or your Father's business (Luke 2:41-52)? Above all else, God's Blueprint for us is one that directs us to cherish our time as a blessing from above. We are called to read His Word, seek His direction in prayer, serve others, and lovingly lead those He has placed in our care. Our lifetimes in this world have expirations, but we are all given enough time to accomplish the work God desires to complete in us. God's timing is perfect.

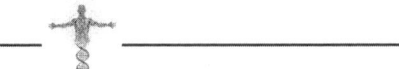

Talents

In his grace, God has given us different gifts for doing certain things well...

Romans 12:6

You are gifted.

You were born with God-designed abilities that set you apart and make you unique. The moment you placed your faith in Christ, the Holy Spirit coupled those genetic gifts with spiritual gifts, making you the perfect vessel for carrying out God's plan for your life.

I've met thousands of different people with thousands of different gifts. I've met people who have natural abilities to cook, play sports, sing, solve problems, make people laugh, decorate, organize, build things, etc. I've met people who are amazing with children. I've had the privilege of working with people like Sam Ellsworth, who can entertain teenagers for hours with a deck of cards. I've met people who literally radiate compassion – it's impossible to talk to them without feeling blessed. I've met people who work extremely hard for days on ministry projects, yet are constantly filled with joy. I've learned and been discipled by individuals gifted in teaching and preaching. I've gained guidance and direction from those blessed with great wisdom. My life has been lifted up by those gifted in prayer. You are gifted.

Consider Christ's Parable of the Three Servants:

> *"Again, the Kingdom of Heaven can be illustrated by the story of a man going on a long trip. He called together his servants and entrusted his money to them while he was*

gone. He gave five bags of silver to one, two bags of silver to another, and one bag of silver to the last—dividing it in proportion to their abilities. He then left on his trip.

"The servant who received the five bags of silver began to invest the money and earned five more. The servant with two bags of silver also went to work and earned two more. But the servant who received the one bag of silver dug a hole in the ground and hid the master's money.

"After a long time their master returned from his trip and called them to give an account of how they had used his money. The servant to whom he had entrusted the five bags of silver came forward with five more and said, 'Master, you gave me five bags of silver to invest, and I have earned five more.'

"The master was full of praise. 'Well done, my good and faithful servant. You have been faithful in handling this small amount, so now I will give you many more responsibilities. Let's celebrate together!'

"The servant who had received the two bags of silver came forward and said, 'Master, you gave me two bags of silver to invest, and I have earned two more.'

"The master said, 'Well done, my good and faithful servant. You have been faithful in handling this small amount, so now I will give you many more responsibilities. Let's celebrate together!'

"Then the servant with the one bag of silver came and said, 'Master, I knew you were a harsh man, harvesting crops you didn't plant and gathering crops you didn't cultivate. I was afraid I would lose your money, so I hid it in the earth. Look, here is your money back.'

"But the master replied, 'You wicked and lazy servant! If you knew I harvested crops I didn't plant and gathered crops I didn't cultivate, why didn't you deposit my *money in the bank? At least I could have gotten some interest on it.'*

"Then he ordered, 'Take the money from this servant, and give it to the one with the ten bags of silver. To those who use well what they are given, even more will be given, and they will have an abundance. But from those who do nothing, even what little they have will be taken away. Now throw this useless servant into outer darkness, where there will be weeping and gnashing of teeth.'"

Matthew 25:14-30

Oddly enough, the word "silver" in this passage is translated from the Greek word meaning "a talent," which was a unit of measurement equal to about 75 pounds (34 kilograms). It is from this Greek word that our modern English word "talent" has its origin.

Although Jesus talks specifically about silver in this illustration, the principle applies to all areas of our blessings, including our gifts and abilities. As we read this parable, our hearts should be stirred with the truth that God desires us to invest our talents in the growth of His Kingdom.

The servant who was given five bags of silver used it to double what was given, and his stewardship was blessed. Despite having less, the servant with the two bags of silver did the same thing. In return he received more responsibilities and the master celebrated his faithfulness.

We can learn a lot from the third servant. He was entrusted with little and he didn't use it. Out of fear, he clung to what little had been entrusted to him, not willing to surrender it for the master's purpose.

What ultimately matters is not how much talent you have, but what you do with the talent that God has given you. Your talent may be small, but if you use it for God's glory, He will multiply it.

God's Blueprint is perfect. You've been blessed with just the right abilities and talents; exactly what you need to bring God glory in your life. If you only have a little bit of talent, use what you have for God's glory, and watch Him take that little bit and do awesome things with it. If you've been blessed with an abundance of talent, you've also been entrusted with great responsibility. Live wisely and pursue God's will in everything.

If you can sing, glorify God with your music. If you can cook, feed others for God's glory by showing them the same love and hospitality He has shown you. If you can play football, play for God's glory by making the football field your mission field. If you love to fish, fish for God's glory by using it to build relationships with others and share the things of God with them. Whatever you do, do it for God's glory (1 Corinthians 10:31).

Are you honoring God with your talents, or using them to bring applause and popularity to yourself? Do you even know what your talents are? The jar of your talents is one that God fills over and over, but only if you surrender to Him. The more you allow Him to use your gifts, the more gifts He will give you.

Finances

Remember this—a farmer who plants only a few seeds will get a small crop. But the one who plants generously will get a generous crop. You must each decide in your heart how much to give. And don't give reluctantly or in response to pressure. "For God loves a person who gives cheerfully."

2 Corinthians 9:6-7

If stewardship is where the rubber meets the road, finances are where the brakes meet the tires.

Money is often the last thing we want to surrender to God. Why?

For the love of money is the root of all kinds of evil. And some people, craving money, have wandered from the true faith and pierced themselves with many sorrows.

1 Timothy 6:10

Money isn't evil, but the love of money is the root of all kinds of evil. If we're not careful, our lives can easily revolve around the bottom dollar. When it comes to fear, money is the devil's greatest enticement to weaken our faith and strip away valuable jars designed to hold abundant blessings.

Although the world is filled with financially wealthy people who hold no regard to God's plan for finances, we must consider the longevity of that wealth. Money on its own has no eternal value, but money blessed by the Architect can accomplish more than we can imagine.

For centuries, people have spoken of the church in a way demeaning its purposes. Sadly, at least some of the bad rap towards the church is deserved. Greedy church leadership, dishonest pastors, and scams of supernatural promises have given many people the perception that church is all about money.

The church is not about money, but if the church is going to thrive and grow, if people in need are going to be helped, and if the gospel is going to reach the outermost parts of the globe, then money is needed. As unspiritual as this may sound, it's the simple reality of the world we live in.

It doesn't matter how much money we have. What matters is how we use the money. The church could have all the money in the world, but if that money isn't being used wisely according to the principles of biblical stewardship, it's all wasted.

How we use our money is determined by how we *view* our money.

- If we view our money as an entitlement for our hard work, we're missing the true rewards of the Rewarder.
- If we view our money as our security for survival, we're missing the provision of the Provider.
- If we view our money as our wealth, we're selling ourselves short of experiencing the ultimate riches of our Heavenly Father.

Our finances can't define our faith.

Our faith must define our finances.

Let me ask two questions: *What do you give? What do you do with what is left over?*

The natural approach is to use our money to please ourselves, then give what is left over to others. After all, we worked hard and earned it! We want to live off the "substance" of our money, and only give from the "excess" (what is left over after we've spent the substance.)

From a purely secular perspective, this seems to make perfect sense. But here's an example of where Jesus takes something that makes sense, and totally flips it upside down. Jesus is too countercultural for "business as usual." The world says "you earned the money, keep it for yourself." But Jesus says:

> *Give to those who ask, and don't turn away from those who want to borrow.*
>
> *Matthew 5:42*

> *When you put on a luncheon or a banquet, don't invite your friends, brothers, relatives, and rich neighbors. For they will invite you back, and that will be your only reward. Instead, invite the poor, the crippled, the lame, and the blind. Then at the resurrection of the righteous, God will reward you for inviting those who could not repay you.*
>
> *Excerpt from Luke 14:12-14*

Jesus calls us to be radically different! If we go back to that story recorded in 2 Kings, the widow did everything Elisha asked and God worked a great miracle. She had a debt to pay, and nothing but a tiny jar of olive oil to pay it with. How could she possibly give when she had so little? She easily could have clung to that jar – literally her last possession – and refused to give it to the man of God. She had every right to do so! But instead, she chose to do something radically different. She willingly surrendered everything she had. The result? An incredible miracle – before her very eyes she saw the olive oil multiply to fill every jar.

> *When she told the man of God what had happened, he said to her, "Now sell the olive oil and pay your debts, and you and your sons can live on what is left over."*
>
> *2 Kings 4:7*

Instead of living off the substance and giving from the excess, she gave away the substance and lived off the excess. She had a great debt to pay, so she took the little bit of blessing she had and paid that first, trusting that God would provide through what was left over.

> *Give, and you will receive. Your gift will return to you in full—pressed down, shaken together to make room for more, running over, and poured into your lap. The amount you give will determine the amount you get back.*
>
> *Luke 6:38*

"Running over, and poured into your lap." This is what God desires. If we learn to give from our substance first, and live off what's left over, God will provide for us in a way that only He can – provision of biblical proportions. Through money, peace, joy, love, reconciliation, grace, lifechange, and worldchange, Jesus Christ promises abundance.

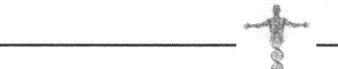

What Should I Give?

You must obediently give from your substance. Proverbs 3:9 tells us this:

> *Honor the LORD with your wealth and with the best part of everything you produce.*

The best part is the first part. When we are considering the stewardship of our finances we have to set aside our giving *first*, then everything else falls into line. Every time I've experienced financial devastation, it was because I devoured the first fruits and only gave what little was left. Don't let this happen to you.

Give first. Ask questions later.

Tithe: There are three ways we can give, the first being the tithe. Our tithe is the required foundation of our financial stewardship. God gives us an awesome principle of giving to anchor our faith in His ability to provide. A tithe, by biblical definition, is ten percent of your financial income.

> *You must set aside a tithe of your crops—**one-tenth** of all the crops you harvest each year.*
>
> *Deuteronomy 14:22*

We give back to God by financially supporting the local church and ministries actively accomplishing His work. To tithe means to give God ten percent of our harvest – in other words, giving ten percent of our income.

That means ten percent of every paycheck, not ten percent of what's left over after we pay the bills. This simple concept may make you uncomfortable, even a bit scared. Why? Because it requires faith. If we trust in money to protect us, giving away ten percent can be pretty intimidating. But if we trust in God as our provider, we can give with joy, knowing that He will take care of us, and multiply the blessings.

We may "lose" ten percent of a paycheck right now, but we'll ultimately gain riches of far greater value. When we faithfully tithe with a cheerful heart, God takes that tithe, uses it to build His Kingdom, and multiplies it back to us in the form of blessings beyond our wildest dreams. That's worth more than any paycheck.

People often tell me, "If we tithe then we won't be able to pay our bills!" I always respond with this question, "Did you faithfully try it?"

If it makes sense, it's probably not faith.

God literally challenges us to test Him in these things.

> *"Bring all the tithes into the storehouse so there will be enough food in my Temple. If you do," says the LORD of Heaven's Armies, "I will open the windows of heaven for you. I will pour out a blessing so great you won't have enough room to take it in! Try it! Put me to the test!"*
>
> *Malachi 3:10*

God isn't messing around. He wants you to take the lid off your finances, relinquish control, and give to Him *first*. If you do, He'll bless you beyond your capacity.

God gives you 100%. You give Him back 10% and keep 90%. Then He turns around and blesses your life beyond your imagination.

This is literally the best deal in the history of the universe!

Why are we so unwilling to do it?

God is essentially saying, "Give it a genuine try, and I promise you'll experience the blessings." This is a guarantee from the Almighty Ruler of the universe. It doesn't get better than that.

Once you start experiencing the blessings, tithing becomes a joy rather than a burden. We should *look forward* to the opportunity to give our ten percent to God. Every time our family experiences financial difficulty, rather than withholding our tithe, I tell my wife, "Don't forget to put our tithe in this week!" Why? Because it's in the hard times that tithing is most important. When we're in dire straits financially, that's when tithing requires the most faith. But it's also when we need God's blessings the most.

<u>Offering</u>: The second way to give is offering. Offering is often confused with the tithe, but the two are not the same. Your tithe is the set amount God requires you to give. Your offering is anything you prayerfully give beyond that.

> *Then celebrate the Festival of Harvest to honor the LORD your God. Bring him a voluntary offering in proportion to the blessings you have received from him.*
>
> *Deuteronomy 16:10*

Notice that the offering is voluntary, and "in proportion to the blessings you have received." While the tithe is a set amount, you choose how much your offering is. An offering is literally an act of worship. It should be done joyfully out of a heart so in love with God that you are not just willing but *longing* to give to His work.

Has God recently helped you through a challenging season in your life? Has He blessed you abundantly in your finances, perhaps with a big promotion? Maybe you're experiencing hardship, but you have such faith that God will provide that you want to surrender what little you have to Him.

Whatever the circumstance, giving an offering is an extraordinary way to praise God for all He is doing in your life.

I remember my dad telling a story one Sunday when I was a young boy. He was giving a testimony about the joys of being obedient. He shared how earlier that morning he had gotten up and was getting ready for church when the devil began to fight him about giving his tithe for the week. He was going through a tough time at his job and was on shaky ground financially. The devil put this thought in his head: "You can't afford to give that much money!"

Right then and there, my dad drew a line in the sand and made a declaration: "I am going to live by faith, not by fear."

In fact, my dad was so moved by God's gentle faithfulness in the middle of that temptation, he decided to give even *more* than his tithe. My dad gave an offering to God that day as a way of saying, "Thank You for Your provision and Your faithfulness. Thank You for being who You are!" He didn't allow the fear of giving to steal his joy.

Not long after that, God blessed my dad with the finances necessary to purchase his first machine for what would become a successful manufacturing business.

An offering is a jar-expanding, faith-strengthening act of worship.

<u>**Alms**</u>: Jesus calls us to feed the hungry, give drink to the thirsty, be hospitable the stranger, clothe the naked, look after the sick, and visit those in prison (Matthew 25:31-46). But *the way* we do these good deeds is just as important as the deeds themselves. In Matthew 6:1-4, Jesus gives us the Blueprint for how we should give to help those in need:

> *Watch out! Don't do your good deeds publicly, to be admired by others, for you will lose the reward from your Father in heaven. When you give to someone in need,*

> *don't do as the hypocrites do—blowing trumpets in the synagogues and streets to call attention to their acts of charity! I tell you the truth, they have received all the reward they will ever get. But when you give to someone in need, don't let your left hand know what your right hand is doing. Give your gifts in private, and your Father, who sees everything, will reward you.*

Alms are the extension of our love that flows from the saving grace of Jesus Christ. Just as He so generously pours out His compassion and blessings to us, so we must do the same to others. What we give to others, our gestures of rescue, and moments of mercy toward others are alms that reflect the cause of the Cross.

Money can't be the anchor – compassion must trump our finances.

> *Teach those who are rich in this world not to be proud and not to trust in their money, which is so unreliable. Their trust should be in God, who richly gives us all we need for our enjoyment. Tell them to use their money to do good. They should be rich in good works and generous to those in need, always being ready to share with others.*
>
> 1 Timothy 6:17-18

What Should I Do with What's Left Over?

You must obediently live off the excess. One of the main reasons many Christians face hardship when it comes to biblical stewardship of finances is a lack of God-centered priorities in this area.

> *Seek the Kingdom of God above all else, and live righteously, and he will give you everything you need.*
>
> Matthew 6:33

Is your financial plan God's financial plan? The definition of stewardship according to Merriam Webster's dictionary is, "The careful and responsible management of something entrusted to one's care."

God calls us to properly manage the financial blessings He places in our care. Once you have given from your substance – your first fruits – what is *left over* is what you actually budget your life around.

We need to have Kingdom-driven priorities when it comes to our money. We need to live within our means and be mindful in determining what is necessary and what is a worldly desire. What do you really need? The Apostle Paul said to Timothy, "If we have enough food and clothing, let us be content" (1 Timothy 6:8).

Stewardship is a call of wisdom-driven management. It requires discipline and humility. The world may boast of its riches and tell you to spend everything on your desires, but Jesus calls us to live in the reality of eternity.

Avoid going into debt, and if you're in debt, work to faithfully pay it off. Don't spend beyond your capacity. Be prayerful in your purchases. Give away your substance. Live off the excess. When the excess is exhausted, we can't extend it beyond what was already given to us. Do you trust God enough to allow Him to bless you with the right amount for exactly what you need, at just the right time? Money is either a blessing to be invested for God's glory or a tool used by the devil to bankrupt your faith.

Relationships

Perhaps the most sensitive "jar" in our lives is our relationships. There are many kinds of relationships. They all require love.

> *Jesus replied, "'You must love the LORD your God with all your heart, all your soul, and all your mind.' This is the first and greatest commandment. A second is equally important: '**Love your neighbor** as yourself.'"*
>
> *Matthew 22:37-39*

Your neighbors are the circle of people you have influence over – the people you rub shoulders with in life. Whether it's at work, at school, at the coffee shop, or even on Facebook, you are called to love your neighbor as you love yourself. Love is reflective. Your love for others reflects your love for God.

There are three key questions we should ask ourselves when it comes to measuring the health of relationships in our lives.

1. *Who's Influencing Whom?* Jesus was a friend of sinners. He dined with corrupt tax collectors and prostitutes. In fact, He was so close to sinners that people often criticized Him for it. And yet, He never sinned. Are you a friend of sinners? You should be, but only if you are the influencer and not the one influenced. Those relationships can either raise others up, or bring you down, depending on who is influencing whom.

2. *Who's Getting the Glory?* "It's not what you know, but who you know." How many times have we heard that? We are often tempted to have relationships for no other reason than personal advantage. In the relationships in your life, who's getting the glory? Are you friends with a certain person simply because of what you can get from them? There have been times in my life when I cultivated relationships simply because I knew what the fallout would be if I didn't. But this is not a love-focused strategy for relationships. Our relationships need to be more about God and less about us. Every relationship is an opportunity to develop a friendship that brings glory to your Heavenly Father. What is the motivation for the relationships in your life?

3. *Do Your Relationships Have Discipleship Qualities?* Many of the relationships we develop are not particularly close or deep. However, some relationships are extremely powerful. When you become close to someone, you become influential. But *how* are you influencing that person? Are you leading that person to a deeper walk with Christ? Is the relationship rooted in spiritual growth?

As iron sharpens iron, so a friend sharpens a friend.

Proverbs 27:17

These three areas are vital to the success of FAVORful relationships in life. Restructuring, reevaluating, and reconsidering the friendships and influences we have in our lives can be an emotional journey. Be prayerful in examining your relationships.

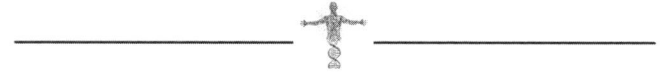

At Odds

Most of us know what it's like to have broken relationships. Perhaps you've experienced bitterness, harsh words, prideful standoffs, gossip, or the pain of regret.

Are you at odds with someone now?

If so, why? How long will it stay that way?

No matter what the circumstances, every broken relationship is broken because of sin. It may be your own sin, the sin of the other person, or even the sin of others. Often, it's a combination of all three.

Anger. Gossip. Jealousy. Pride. Lust. These sins kill relationships on contact.

The good news is this: Every broken relationship can be repaired. You might never be as close to that person as you once were, but you *can* reach a place of forgiveness. You know you've reached that place when you can think about that person and no longer feel bitter inside. Until then, there is work to be done.

If you're at odds with someone, don't allow the relationship to remain broken. Don't allow bitter feelings to fester inside of you. Take action. Search your heart. Seek them out. Forgive them. Settle the matter.

It won't be easy. It will require humility, grace, and plenty of strength. But Jesus Christ is the provider of these gifts and He gives them freely. If you're finding it hard to forgive someone, repent of the unforgiveness you're holding in your heart, and ask God to help you forgive.

Forgiveness is not optional – it's a direct command from the Lord Jesus Christ (Matthew 6:14-15). You might say, "But they don't *deserve* to be forgiven!" That may be true. But consider this: You didn't deserve to be forgiven of your sins, yet Jesus Christ forgave you anyway. He asks you to take the same unmerited grace He gave you, and extend it to others. Ultimately, forgiving others is for our own benefit. Withholding forgiveness is like grasping a hot coal. The longer we hold onto those feelings of bitterness, the more they burn us. The pain slowly destroys us from within. The only way to be free from it is to let go. Christian author Lewis B. Smedes said, "To forgive is to set a prisoner free and discover that the prisoner was you."

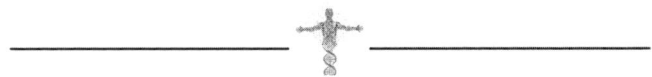

Daily Surrender

Being a Christian requires daily surrender. In a paradox that only God could have orchestrated, surrender actually produces victory. God doesn't want us to surrender because He's a heavenly control freak. He loves us and knows what our hearts passionately beat for.

> *Take delight in the LORD, and he will give you your heart's desires. Commit everything you do to the LORD. Trust him, and he will help you.*
>
> *Psalm 37:4-5*

The phrase "take delight" is translated from the Hebrew word *anag*, meaning "to be soft or pliable." Surrendering is not about losing. It's about yielding to the Sculptor so He can shape us into a masterpiece. As long as we keep trying to do things our own way, our desires will always be just out of reach. But when we give our time, talents, finances, and relationships to God, He fills these jars to overflowing.

Are you ready to begin each day by surrendering?

Thoughts from Chapter 6: Jars

Time. Talents. Finances. Relationships. These are four areas of your life your Heavenly Father desires to abundantly bless! Biblical stewardship means understanding that everything you have ultimately belongs to God. You must surrender ownership and take borrowship. Seek God's will for your time rather than scheduling your life around your own desires. Use your talents to build God's Kingdom. Give from your substance and live off the excess. Forgive others and build relationships with discipleship qualities.

Questions to Consider

Do you believe God can manage your time, talents, finances, and relationships better than you can? In each of these areas, are you living by faith or fear?

Think about how your time is scheduled on a typical day. How much is spent pursuing God's will? Are you too busy with your own agenda?

What are your gifts? How are you using those gifts for God's glory?

Are you managing your finances biblically, giving (tithe, offering, alms) from your substance and living off the excess?

In what condition are the relationships in your life? Are you at odds with someone? Who is getting the glory in your relationships? Do your relationships have discipleship qualities?

Additional Verses to Study / How Can i Apply This?

- Matthew 6:24-34

- 1 Timothy 6:17-19

- Galatians 6:7-9

- Proverbs 16

- Matthew 18:21-35

Building Blocks: Before i Move On...

☐ I surrender ownership of my life to God, and take borrowship.

☐ God has given me exactly what I need to accomplish His purpose in my life.

☐ In my time, talents, finances, and relationships I will live by faith, not by fear.

☐ I am biblically tithing ten percent of my income to my local church.

Prayer

Heavenly Father, everything I have is from You. I only have borrowship of my life, not ownership. I surrender my time, talents, finances, and relationships to You. You can handle these things better than I can, and I ask for Your will to be done in these areas of my life. Give me wisdom to understand Your will for my life, and the boldness to accomplish it. Help me to schedule my time according to Your will, and rest in a moment-by-moment relationship with You. Please help me to use every gift you've given me to build Your Kingdom. Help me to fearlessly give from my substance to bless others and sustain the local church. Help me to extend to others the same radical mercy that You have shown me. Amen.

CHAPTER 7
HOMELAND SECURITY

The Flaming Marshmallow

"Our culture has accepted two huge lies. The first is that if you disagree with someone's lifestyle, you must fear or hate them. The second is that to love someone means you agree with everything they believe or do. Both are nonsense. You don't have to compromise convictions to be compassionate."

-Rick Warren, Senior Pastor of Saddleback Church

I've been eager to write this chapter for a long time. I won't tiptoe around or pull any punches. I've seen too many families fall apart, too many kids suffer, and too many churches crumble because of homes in devastation. I'm convicted to share what God has faithfully shown me over years of marriage. Through all of the ups and downs, God faithfully guided my wife Theresa and me through some painful steps of growth, but today our home is healthier for it.

Whether you're a teenager feeling misunderstood at home, a young adult looking for spouse to build a home with, a parent with children, or a retiree enjoying your golden years – we can all agree that "there's no place like home." We all have much to learn about God's design for the home. While the home may seem mundane and at times unimportant, the reality is that the home has eternal significance. The way we run our households not only affects us, but shapes the next generation.

When I was growing up, my family had a tradition of camping one week at a campsite about an hour from our house. I always looked forward to it every summer. We would swim, ride bikes, chop firewood, feed chipmunks, and eat the finest campfire food you could imagine.

One particular year there was an evening when we were all sitting by the fire roasting marshmallows and making smores. My sister, Tonya, was toasting a marshmallow and got it a little too close to the fire. Almost immediately her marshmallow went into flames. She pulled it out and blew on it, putting out the flames – or so she thought. Although it looked like the flames were out, the other side of the marshmallow was still burning. She reached up to pull it off the stick and burned her fingers. In our family, this became known as "the incident of the flaming marshmallow."

Is your home a flaming marshmallow?

Some households are clearly "on fire" – there is chaos and dysfunction everywhere, and the problems are obvious for all to see. However, in many homes the problems lay under the surface. While everything appears good on the outside, there are flames burning in the background. We blow on one side of the marshmallow with temporary whispers, adding new philosophies to ease our minds, but we are in a crisis situation. There are serious problems that need real solutions.

But really, isn't everyone's family like that? Doesn't every family have issues? Isn't that normal?

As a culture, we've become so used to dysfunctional families that they don't seem dysfunctional anymore. Healthy families are strangely absent from modern television, while broken and chaotic homes are celebrated. Our culture has abandoned God's Blueprint for the home. Instead of dealing with serious problems, we use the excuse "times have changed." Messed up is the new normal.

The Big Mac Mentality

"But if you refuse to serve the LORD, then choose today whom you will serve. Would you prefer the gods your ancestors served beyond the Euphrates? Or will it be the gods of the Amorites in whose land you now live? But as for me and my family, we will serve the LORD."

Joshua 24:15

We all know the story of Moses leading the Israelites out of slavery in Egypt and parting the Red Sea. However, many people don't realize that it wasn't just happily-ever-after from that point on. The Israelites repeatedly disobeyed God and even sought to return to Egypt. When they finally made it to the Promised Land, they refused to go in! God had given them this amazing land of great abundance, but instead of taking possession of it, they wandered in the wilderness for 40 years because of their unbelief.

After the death of Moses, God appointed Joshua to lead the people into the Promised Land. Joshua was dealing with a stubborn group of people who struggled to believe and obey God, even after witnessing incredible miracles. In the verse quoted above, Joshua essentially said to them, "Look, I know there are a whole bunch of other 'gods' you could worship. There are all kinds of idols. There are all kinds of philosophies and ideas. You can go ahead and believe whatever you want. But as for me and my family, we're serving the LORD. We're following the Blueprint."

In the old days, McDonald's served only the few items that were on the menu – nothing more, nothing less. There were no "value meals," no "dollar menu," no fancy salads made to order, and there was definitely no such thing as a McCafé Frappé Mocha with whipped cream and caramel drizzle.

Then Burger King started offering custom orders, meaning you could literally tell them to add extra ketchup but hold the onions. Remember those old "Have It Your Way at BK" commercials?

Well, McDonald's had to follow suit, and now fast food places everywhere offer customized menu options. In fact, it's the new normal. We want to get exactly what we want, when we want it. We want all of life to be the same – "customizable" according to our desires. Our culture has an addiction to instant gratification. Go into McDonald's today and you can order a grilled chicken sandwich with Swiss cheese, shredded lettuce, Big Mac sauce, and bacon, and get it delivered in a chicken nugget box. Whatever you want, you can have.

The home is **NOT** that way.

The home is *not* customizable according to *your* desires.

We live in a culture that hates absolutes. The world tells us there is no right or wrong way to raise a family – it's "whatever" works for you.

Let me tell you, as clearly and directly as I can, that this kind of thinking is simply wrong. There *are* absolutes. Not every family is going to be the same, but there are things that work, and things that don't work. There are godly principles guaranteed to produce blessings and joy. There are also things that are toxic to the home, guaranteed to produce broken relationships, bitterness, and pain.

In the pages of the Bible, God gives us a specific Blueprint for the home. Our culture may tell us that there is no right or wrong way to do marriage, parenting, and sex. But God's Word declares absolutes, not "whatevers."

Do you know God's plan for your marriage? Do you know His will for your children? Have you stopped to consider that your relationship with your partner may be outside of God's design? God desires to anoint your family with abundant blessings. He *wants* you to have an amazing, passionate sex life. He's excited about what your home can be! He can heal wounds of pain and distrust. He can help guide a wayward child. Your Heavenly Father can saturate your home with a love that overcomes all obstacles. But God can't bless our homes if we stubbornly refuse to surrender them to Him.

The Foundation

> *So now you Gentiles are no longer strangers and foreigners. You are citizens along with all of God's holy people. You are members of God's family. Together, we are his house, built on the foundation of the apostles and the prophets. And the cornerstone is Christ Jesus himself. We are carefully joined together in him, becoming a holy temple for the Lord. Through him you Gentiles are also being made part of this dwelling where God lives by his Spirit.*
>
> Ephesians 2:19-22

The most important part of a building is not the roof, the walls, or even the floor. The most important part is the foundation. More than anything else, the strength of the foundation is what determines whether the building stands or falls. When tall skyscrapers are built, the first step is to reinforce the ground with concrete and steel. Before the first brick or girder is ever laid into place, the foundation must be prepared.

When Theresa and I were looking to buy a house, we learned that a good foundation is hard to find! House after house, the realtor would take us into the basement and we would find walls shifting, columns heaving, and blocks crumbling. No matter how fancy a house is on the outside, it's not worth much if it's built on a weak foundation.

Jesus echoes these thoughts in Matthew 7:24-27.

> *"Anyone who listens to my teaching and follows it is wise, like a person who builds a house on solid rock. Though the rain comes in torrents and the floodwaters rise and the winds beat against that house, it won't collapse because it is built on bedrock. But anyone who hears my teaching and doesn't obey it is foolish, like a person who builds a house on sand. When the rains and floods come and the winds beat against that house, it will collapse with a mighty crash."*

The foundation of our home must be the teachings of the apostles and prophets as recorded in God's Word and ultimately culminating with Jesus Christ, the chief cornerstone upon which everything else depends.

Jesus Christ is the Redeemer, the Healer, the Savior, the Grace-giver, the Resurrection, and the Life. He is the Rock that God calls us to build our families upon.

As a pastor, I've counseled hundreds of people struggling with marriage and parenting. Although each situation is unique, at the core it's always the same problem: Jesus Christ is not the foundation of the home.

Work, money, time, entertainment, laziness, past emotional baggage, pride, and a million other things can easily replace Jesus Christ in our homes.

Is Jesus Christ the foundation of your home? Is He the cornerstone that everything else in your home rests on? Is your family faithfully pursuing a daily relationship with Him?

When my family and I are reading God's Word, praying, and praising together, we are bound together with unbreakable cords. It reinforces the foundation of our family, strengthens us, and gives me confidence as a father.

God designed our homes to be built on Jesus Christ because His supernatural attributes empower us to hold it all together. Our families are made up of imperfect people, but God's grace reigns in and through Jesus Christ to cover a multitude of sins. He is the solid rock that secures us through the fiercest storms. He is the guarantee of victory no matter the circumstance. If your home is not rooted in the Word and anchored in the Rock, your home is on sinking sand.

The Front Door Of Love

We know how much God loves us, and we have put our trust in his love. God is love, and all who live in love live in God, and God lives in them.

1 John 4:16

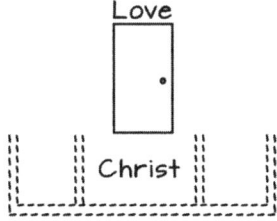

Is God's love for you real? Does it take your breath away?

Is the fact that Jesus Christ died for you – your brother, your sister, your husband, your wife, your children – a reality in your life?

> *Love is patient and kind. Love is not jealous or boastful or proud or rude. It does not demand its own way. It is not irritable, and it keeps no record of being wronged. It does not rejoice about injustice but rejoices whenever the truth wins out. Love never gives up, never loses faith, is always hopeful, and endures through every circumstance.*
>
> 1 Corinthians 13:4-7

The front door of the home must be a door of love – His love. The closer your family is to God, the more His love is manifested in your family.

Imagine a household driven by supernatural love – a place where patience is practiced and kindness is the norm, where grudges aren't kept and no one is easily irritated. Imagine a family bound together in perfect love - a family that never gives up and never loses faith. Wouldn't you love to be part of that family?

Okay, back to reality.

It's been two days of working late and your youngest child just poured an entire gallon of milk on the floor because he wanted cereal and you weren't around because you're busy working the checkbook and just realized you have a balance of $46.98 in your account with $300 worth of bills to pay. Your car needs new tires and your teenage daughter just started chatting with a boy who you think would make a great throw rug. The shingles on the roof are getting bad and you just stubbed your toe on the same nail sticking up on that threshold that's been there for three months even though it would only take 45 seconds to pound it back in....

Guess what? Even in the midst of all that chaos, your home can still be infused with love. A family driven by love is not a family free of problems. Having a "front door of love" doesn't mean we will never experience difficulties, struggles, or arguments. It's how we respond to these challenges that determines if love reigns supreme in our households or not.

> *Three things will last forever—faith, hope, and love—and the greatest of these is love.*
>
> 1 Corinthians 13:13

Do you realize how *important* love is? Love is the substance of faith and hope. God's love will do more for your home than Oprah could ever do.

God's love can accomplish more in one day than years of counseling. God's love is healing. God's love is faithful. God's love is securing.

God's love is greater than the enemy's attacks on your family – even greater than anything this world has to offer. I'm not saying this with the attitude of "I'm perfect," but rather, "I've been there." The love of God literally saved my marriage. Years ago, my family made a proclamation to live for God. Ever since, His love has transformed everything. It didn't happen overnight. But a family's hunger for God is like a sponge. As we seek Him, we soak up His love so when we're pressed by challenge, love is what pours out. Love always wins.

Experiencing God's love in your home is more than just having a quick family meeting and saying "I love you," when the kids run off to bed. God's love works from the inside out. His love transforms whole families by transforming individual hearts. It starts with a family's commitment to live for Him.

It's a daily pursuit that pursues us daily.

The Walls of Obedience

If you love me, obey my commandments.

John 14:15

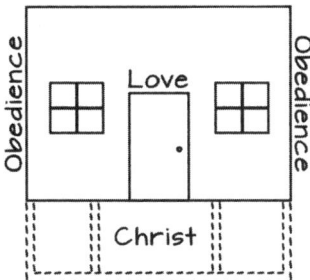

If the front door to a healthy home is love, then the walls are built of obedience. God gives us commandments to protect us from the pain and adversity that sin causes. A home immersed in God's love is one obediently living according to the Blueprint.

> *Study this Book of Instruction continually. Meditate on it day and night so you will be sure to obey everything written in it. Only then will you prosper and succeed in all you do.*
>
> Joshua 1:8

God designed the home to be wrapped in the pavilion of His Word. The walls of His commandments keep what's good inside the home and keep what's harmful out. Having a powerful understanding of the Blueprint is critical to the health and safety of your household.

Sin can destroy what God desires to elevate. Sin can manipulate your marriage and corrupt your children. God calls us to study His Word, build up the walls of His commandments, and obediently hold them in place. Are your walls strong?

> *Listen, O Israel! The LORD is our God, the LORD alone. And you must love the LORD your God with all your heart, all your soul, and all your strength. And you must commit yourselves wholeheartedly to these commands that I am giving you today. Repeat them again and again to your children. Talk about them when you are at home and when you are on the road, when you are going to bed and when you are getting up. Tie them to your hands and wear them on your forehead as reminders. Write them on the doorposts of your house and on your gates.*
>
> Deuteronomy 6:4-9

Does your family regularly spend time together in God's Word? Do you repeat His Word to your children "again and again"? Do you talk about His Blueprint when you're at home and when you're on the road, when you go to bed and when you get up? Is God's Word written on the doorposts of your home? Are you constantly reminded of His promises?

Are you continually teaching your children to live by the Blueprint? Are you obediently living out the commands God has given you?

For many years, the "walls" of my home were no more than a few pages high. I breezed through the Bible, cherry picking the verses I liked while ignoring the rest. I believed that Christ died for me, but I wasn't serious about living for Him. I memorized His promises, but not His commandments. My family and I lived with no boundaries. I rarely prayed and never sought God's will. I wanted to structure my home according to my own design. I wanted to "have it my way."

Because I never put the walls of obedience in place, my home was vulnerable to the relentless attacks of devil (1 Peter 5:8). Amazingly, I didn't even realize it at the time. Sin is subtle. If we're not careful, sin has a way of creeping up on us so slowly we don't even see it's there. My children were being polluted and I didn't even realize it. The fact that my marriage was falling apart never even registered until it was almost too late. We had no walls of obedience to keep the bad stuff out and the good stuff in.

Our homes cannot prosper until we build the walls of obedience. Without those walls in place, there is no protection against the enemy. Greed, pride, pornography, violence, alcohol, gossip, grudges, and the workaholic syndrome are all Blueprint killers that creep up on us if our walls are not secure.

How are your walls? What is the centerpiece of your life, your family, and your home? Is it God's Word? What are you letting into your home? What are you keeping out?

The Roof of Biblical Marriage

Then the LORD God said, "It is not good for the man to be alone. I will make a helper who is just right for him." So the LORD God formed from the ground all the wild animals and all the birds of the sky. He brought them to the man to see what he would call them, and the man chose a name for each one. He gave names to all the livestock, all the birds of the sky, and all the wild animals. But still there was no helper just right for him. So the LORD God caused the man to fall into a deep sleep. While the man slept, the LORD God took out one of the man's ribs and closed up the opening. Then the LORD God made a woman from the rib, and he brought her to the man. "At last!" the man exclaimed. "This one is bone from my bone, and flesh from my flesh! She will be called 'woman,' because she was taken from 'man.'" This explains why a man leaves his father and mother and is joined to his wife, and the two are united into one.

Genesis 2:18-24

This is the official start of what God originally ordained as a biblical marriage. A biblical marriage is the only adequate roof over any family's home. We live in a culture that is redefining marriage to include different forms and preferences, but God still remains the Creator of marriage, and His design for it is the only standard for biblical marriage. His Blueprint is not open for revision. God's Blueprint is perfect. We simply need to accept it, and live by it.

For the sinful nature is always hostile to God. It never did obey God's laws, and it never will.

Romans 8:7

This isn't about being judgmental or confrontational. This is about protecting something beautiful and divinely ordained as good. Unfortunately, many Christians are accused of being hateful toward those who choose a different lifestyle. And sadly, there are some so-called Christians who are driven by hatred and lack Christ-like compassion. I want you to know that that's *not* the case in this book. My desire here is not to attack anyone, but simply to elevate God's design for marriage. I won't hate you if you disagree. In fact, my compassion, concern, and love for you won't change one bit if you disagree. But understand that God's Blueprint doesn't change just because culture changes. Remember the quote that opened this chapter: *You don't have to compromise convictions to be compassionate.*

God defines marriage as being between a man and a woman, living under His authority. Anything outside of that is sin and God simply can't bless it because it's not the way He designed it to be. God said it wasn't good for Adam to be alone. God acknowledged that Adam needed a companion – a wife. Marriage has a triangular structure that actually requires *three* individuals: a man, a woman, and God.

For me, Genesis 2 is incredibly moving. Adam needed a wife to complete him. God saw the need and provided the love of Adam's life. Not only that, but He perfectly united them into one. Marriage is awesome. Although no marriage is perfect, a biblical marriage is perfectly imperfect. Marriage is the roof of the home, and when all three points of the roof are working correctly, marriage is nothing short of miraculous.

> *For wives, this means submit to your husbands as to the Lord. For a husband is the head of his wife as Christ is the head of the church. He is the Savior of his body, the church. As the church submits to Christ, so you wives should submit to your husbands in everything.*
>
> *Ephesians 5:22-24*

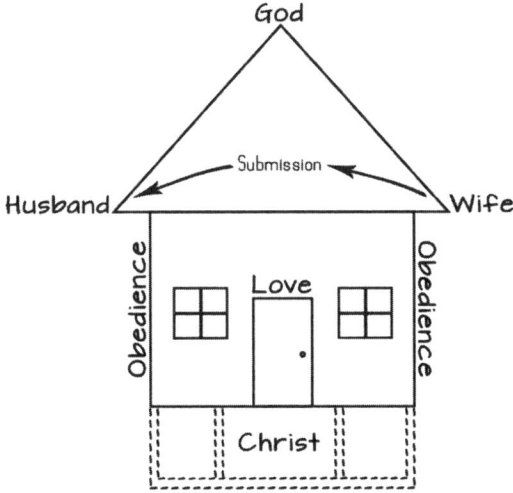

Sadly, this is one of the most abused and twisted passages in the Bible. I've been to many Bible studies where this passage was looked at. Without fail, there's always a woman who says something like, "That's ridiculous! I would never submit to a man!"

In recent years there has been a great decrease in godly men, and we are beginning to see the effects of this on society. Statistics show a continual increase in absentee fathers. More and more children are growing up without fathers in the home, either because of divorce or because their dads simply aren't around. Fewer and fewer men are remaining faithful in marriage – more and more are choosing not to get married at all. Studies show that children who grow up without a strong father figure are less likely to do well in school, and more likely to do drugs or commit crimes. More and more women are faced with raising children on their own because men have failed to do their job.

Although there are still good men out there, it's safe to say that men have failed to be everything God has called them to be. As a result, many women have been hurt, misled, abused, and neglected. Children are growing up without fathers and mothers are living without husbands. Boys are lacking a strong role model for living as a man of God. Girls are looking for attention in all the wrong places because they don't feel loved by their fathers. This is *not* how God designed it. He designed marriage to be led by a man committed in his walk with God. A man who loves God is a man who can be followed passionately. A wife submitting to her husband is not forfeiting her individuality, but embracing the oneness she shares with her husband.

The word for "helper" found in Genesis 2:18 doesn't mean "servant." It means "counterpart." Submission is a divine balance in which a wife allows her husband – who is surrendered to the Lord – to lead the household with God's best interest for her life in perfect focus. When both the husband and the wife are obedient to the Blueprint, the roof of the home is defined by a marriage in perfect partnership.

Submission does *not* mean a man can do whatever he wants and boss his wife around. The husband must submit himself completely to the Lord. The husband must seek the Lord's will above all else. A marriage where the husband selfishly abuses his authority is not healthy, and is completely outside of God's design. But in the same way, a marriage where the wife is constantly fighting for control of the wheel is not healthy either. God specifically designed men to be leaders, protectors, and providers. A wife must allow her husband to live out his calling.

> *The man who finds a wife finds a treasure, and he receives favor from the LORD.*
>
> *Proverbs 18:22*

A godly wife is a treasure of incredible value. God's Blueprint declares favor over the bonds of marriage. Just as an engagement ring holds a diamond, every husband is called to protect his wife, who is his precious jewel. When a wife surrenders to that kind of husbandship, she is elevated in a way that makes her shine.

> *For husbands, this means love your wives, just as Christ loved the church. He gave up his life for her to make her holy and clean, washed by the cleansing of God's word. He did this to present her to himself as a glorious church without a spot or wrinkle or any other blemish. Instead, she will be holy and without fault. In the same way, husbands ought to love their wives as they love their own bodies. For a man who loves his wife actually shows love for himself. No one hates his own body but feeds and cares for it, just as Christ cares for the church. And we are members of his body.*
>
> *Ephesians 5:25-30*

The BLUEPRiNT | 171

The reason many women don't want to submit to their husbands is because too many men are failing to be the husbands God is calling them to be. A wife's submission happens naturally *if* a husband is actively sacrificing himself for her.

Although the command for wives to submit to their husbands may seem demanding, the command for husbands to love their wives is even more demanding. Why? Because husbands are commanded to love their wives "just as Christ loved the church."

Jesus Christ loved the Church enough to die for her. Similarly, a husband must love his wife with everything he has – even giving up his entire life for her.

Frankly, most problems in the home are the husband's fault. Although some problems are caused by wives, I would estimate 90% of problems in the home are caused by husbands simply not loving their wives as Christ loves the Church.

If you're a husband, you probably love your wife. But do you love her *as Christ loved the church?* There is a huge difference between human "love" and the kind of infinite, worldchanging, supernatural love that Jesus Christ demonstrated on the Cross. You are commanded to love your wife with that kind of love.

It's time to man up.

Too many men are wrapped up in collecting toys, gazing at legs, late nights with bands and bottles, conquering the corporate ladder, and fulfilling desires of their flesh.

We need Joshuas!

We need men of courage who are fully surrendered and committed to the Blueprint, who will stand firm on God's Word and not give in to the political-correctness of our culture; men who are going to fearlessly lead their families into the Promised Land, no matter what.

We need men of faithfulness who will go above and beyond what is required to show incredible romance to their wives and be outstanding role models for their children.

We need men to quit settling for the bare minimum and *put in the effort* to be all God calls them to be!

> *Be on guard. Stand firm in the faith. Be courageous. Be strong. And do everything with love.*
>
> 1 Corinthians 16:13-14

The phrase "be courageous" is translated from the Greek word *andrizomai*, which literally means "act manly!"

What does it mean to "act manly?" As men we build castles and surround ourselves with trucks, guns, bacon, beer, money, and Harleys. We pridefully think of ourselves as being tough, manly, and strong. But from the perspective of the God who raised up mountains and carved out canyons, we're nothing more than boys with tricycles.

Boys are primarily concerned with collecting toys and fulfilling their own desires. A *man* surrenders his desires to God. You see, a man's faith is what makes him a real man. His faith in the God of infinite power makes him strong. A real man loves his wife and is actively involved in leading his home and raising his children well.

Are you a real man?

> *When I was a child, I spake as a child, I understood as a child, I thought as a child: but when I became a man, I put away childish things.*
>
> 1 Corinthians 13:11 KJV

It's time to grow up. It's time to get serious, stop "playing church," and start living boldly for Jesus Christ. Boldness starts with a man's God-fearing leadership of the home, standing firm on the principles of God's Word no matter what.

Being a godly husband is a challenging task. It's no place for boys. It's a position of great weight and eternal purpose. It takes a real man to tackle that kind of responsibility.

God calls men to be more than muscle, more than money, and more than mistresses.

Men are called to be *movers* – actively changing their homes and the world for Christ.

> *So humble yourselves before God. Resist the devil, and he will flee from you.*
>
> *James 4:7*

Wives, passionately follow your husbands as they lead.

Husbands, love your wives in a way that lifts her up.

Husbands and wives, surrender yourselves to God.

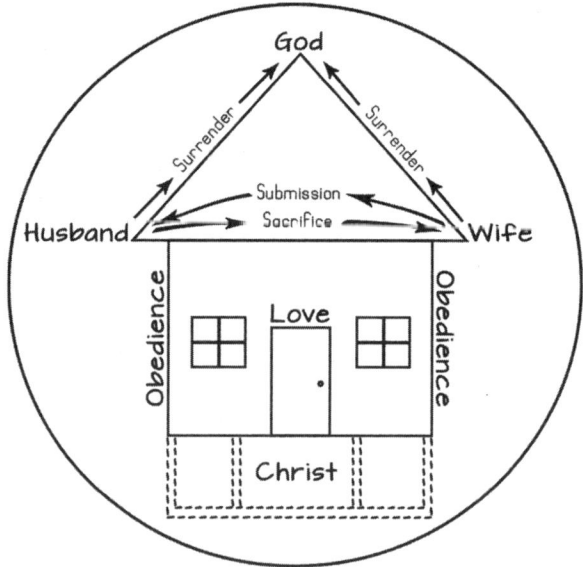

This biblical formula produces a circle that encompasses a blessed home. If we structure our homes in ways that are obedient and faithful to the Author, the devil will have no power over them. He will run.

Every parent should embrace this promise:

> *Direct your children onto the right path, and when they are older, they will not leave it.*
>
> *Proverbs 22:6*

A marriage surrendered to God will train, raise, and direct children on the right path. This is a parent's foremost responsibility. Our homes should be places of spiritual development. Our homes should exude obedience, truth, love, sacrifice, and the relentless mercy-filled power of the Gospel.

What changes do you need to make in your home?

Husbands, what changes do you need to make to man up, love your wife as Christ loved the Church, and be the leader God has called you to be?

Wives, what changes do you need to make to support your husband's God-given role of leadership?

The Bedroom

Give honor to marriage, and remain faithful to one another in marriage. God will surely judge people who are immoral and those who commit adultery.

Hebrews 13:4

If you take the time to study this passage in-depth, you'll find that it's essentially making two points: "Sex inside of marriage is undefiled, but sex outside of marriage is sinful and worthy of judgment."

If you are in a sexual relationship outside of marriage, it's sin and God can't bless it. God created sex for marriage, and only for marriage.

"But we love each other!" That's great, but sex outside of marriage is still sin. If you are really serious about your love for each other, live it out in the unity of marriage.

Unfortunately, we live in a culture where "living together" outside of marriage is a popular and socially acceptable approach to starting a "home." It may be common, but the roofs of those "homes" are badly damaged. Without a marriage commitment giving you the assurance that you will stay together in good times and bad, "till death do us part," you are simply *hoping* to stay together. Without any assurance, you'll feel pressured to perform well, or the other person might leave. The relationship is based on insecurity, and that's no way to start a home. If you're raising children in a cohabiting-but-unmarried relationship, you're not only hurting yourself but putting the children at risk also.

It simply doesn't work.

"But we've already started and it's so good. What are we suppose to do?"

Stop.

It's that simple.

Stop and structure yourselves according to God's Blueprint.

I recently married a young couple, Devin and Trisha. They came to me as new believers who wanted get married but were already sexually active in their relationship. After a couple of hours discussing God's plan for marriage, they made a commitment to remain sexually pure until their wedding day – seven months later. Month by month, day by day, Devin and Trisha's relationship grew and was strengthened in the Lord. God gave them the discipline to complete their task and their love multiplied more than they ever thought possible. Favor is found in the freedom of a surrendered relationship.

Sex is for the marriage bed.

Sex is also for the marriage couch, backseat, coffee table, or shower. Why do Christians have this bad rap of being "prude"? Let me be the first to tell you that's simply not true. As believers, we're called to honor sex by reserving it for marriage. But inside of marriage, sex is open for whatever you can dream up. As long as it involves the husband and wife alone, sex should be free, fun, and completely open to creativity.

"Yeah, but can we…?"

If you're married, the answer is yes.

Fore-play, roll-play, toy-play – the marriage bed is undefiled. God designed sex with one boundary: The boundary of marriage. Sex was designed to enjoy and invigorate.

Where did we get this idea that sex is inherently bad, or "dirty"? As long as sex is within the confines of marriage, *sex is inherently good!* God Himself created it and designed it. He *wants* you to have a great sex life! The passion that comes from a God-centered marriage simply adds to the experience.

It's a perfect passion purposed for pleasure.

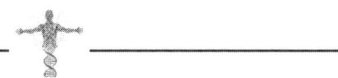

Who Are You Yoking With?

> Don't **team up** with those who are unbelievers. How can righteousness be a partner with wickedness? How can light live with darkness? What harmony can there be between Christ and the devil? How can a believer be a partner with an unbeliever?
>
> 2 Corinthians 6:14-15

Closing out this chapter is a challenge. I realize that 1,000 people could be in a 1,000 different circumstances when it comes to their home, marriage, and relationships.

Maybe you're a husband who's trying to lead, but your wife isn't a believer, and the struggle for a Blueprinted home is daunting.

Maybe you're a wife desperately trying to raise your children according to the Blueprint, but your husband is not supporting your efforts. Take hope in knowing that God is a God of grace.

> For the Christian wife brings holiness to her marriage, and the Christian husband brings holiness to his marriage. Otherwise, your children would not be holy, but now they are holy.
>
> 1 Corinthians 7:14

God sees your desire to have a home centered on Him. Although sin may bring struggles and hardships, your faith has a sanctifying power on your home. Don't lose heart. Pray and lift your spouse before the Redeemer Whose Spirit draws the lost to the foot of the Cross. Press on with humility and love. God is able to do great things with your testimony. Faithfully walk in His Way.

Are you looking to start a home? Take heed to 2 Corinthians 6:14-15. God's perfect design is for you to marry a faithful follower of Jesus Christ. The phrase "team up" literally means "be unequally yoked together" in the original text.

At this point you're probably wondering, "What in the world is a yoke?"

This isn't about eggs. It's about oxen. A yoke is a wooden beam placed over the shoulders of two oxen so they can both pull a plow or wagon together. Both oxen need to be equally strong or the stronger one will pull ahead and wear itself out trying to drag the weaker one behind. You would never yoke an ox with a sheep – that would be ridiculous.

Before you start a home, consider your teammate. Will you be equally yoked? If your response is "He isn't a believer, but he's a good guy," then do NOT become attached to him.

If your response is, "She's not a believer yet, but I think I can lead her to the Lord," then do so, but don't become too intimately yoked to her until she genuinely shares your faith with an equal passion.

Who are you yoking with?

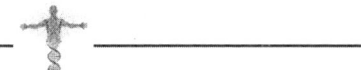

How is Your Home?

As with all other areas of life, God's Blueprint for the home is specific and purposeful. Home is the refuge where we start and end each day. It was never designed to be a struggle, but rather a place of peace and fulfillment. A Blueprinted home is designed to experience the riches of the Architect.

What can you do to seek out God's will for your home?

Thoughts from Chapter 7: Homeland Security

Society is continually redefining "the new normal" for the home. But God's Word teaches truths guaranteed to bring blessings and fulfillment to the home. Your home must be built upon the foundation of Jesus Christ, with a front door of love, walls of obedience, and a roof of biblical marriage. Wives must allow their husbands to live out their God-given call to lead the home. Husbands must love their wives with the same radical, sacrificial love Christ demonstrated on the Cross. Sex is not dirty, but something God designed to be passionately enjoyed and explored inside of marriage. A home structured by the Blueprint not only blesses that family, but shapes the next generation and changes the world.

Questions to Consider

Is your home dysfunctional? If so, are you accepting it as "the new normal" or working to fix it?

What is the foundation of your home? Is Jesus Christ the cornerstone?

Is the front door of your home a door of love? What can you do to pursue God more passionately so His love is what pours out when life presses?

Is there evidence of disobedience to God's Word in your home? Are you teaching your children to live by the Blueprint? Read Deuteronomy 6:4-9.

In what condition is your home's roof of biblical marriage? What can you do to make it stronger? What role does God play in your marriage?

For wives: Are you actively helping your husband fulfill his God-given call to lead the home? Are you a godly counterpart who makes the home complete?

For husbands: Are you actively leading your home under God's authority? Are you loving your wife with sacrificial love, as Christ loved the Church? Are you actively involved in raising your children and teaching them to live by the Blueprint? Are you a Joshua?

For married couples: Is your sex life passionate and fulfilling? Are you enjoying the freedom of exploring the dynamics of sex as God intended? Are there things in your marriage that are robbing you of the fullness of sex's passionate purpose (e.g. pornography, misplaced lust, unfaithfulness, etc.)?

For unmarried people: Who are you yoking with? Are you in a relationship with someone who does not share your passion and love for Jesus Christ? If so, what are you going to do about it?

Additional Verses to Study / How Can i Apply This?

- Ecclesiastes 4:7-12

- Song of Songs 4 (also known as Song of Solomon)

- Psalm 127:3-5

- Ephesians 6:1-4

Building Blocks: Before i Move On…

☐ I believe that God has an absolute Blueprint for the home. The home is not customizable according to my desires.

☐ I have identified changes I need to make to structure my home according to the Blueprint. I am committed to making these changes.

☐ I believe that God designed sex for marriage. I am committed to enjoying sex only inside of marriage.

☐ I am committed to daily teaching my children to live by the Blueprint.

☐ I am committed to being equally yoked in my relationships.

Prayer

Heavenly Father, I praise you for the gift of the home. Please help me to do my part in structuring my home according to Your Blueprint. May my home be built on the foundation of Jesus Christ, with a front door of love, walls of obedience, and a roof of biblical marriage. Please give me the wisdom to identify the changes I need to make in my home to bring it into agreement with Your Blueprint, and empower me to make those changes. Amen.

CHAPTER 8
THE NOT-SO-SUNDAY CHURCH

God has put all things under the authority of Christ and has made him head over all things for the benefit of the church. And the church is his body; it is made full and complete by Christ, who fills all things everywhere with himself.

Ephesians 1:22-23

"Here is the church and here is the steeple. Open the door and see all the people." Remember this nursery rhyme?

The devil isn't afraid of "church." It doesn't bother him too much when Christians sit in pews, sing Christmas carols, play bingo, or have a potluck dinner.

Satan would be perfectly happy with a world full of "churchgoers."

There is a common misconception among Christians that "church" is a weekly event. There's a prevailing mentality that Sunday morning is the time we set aside to honor God. However we live the rest of the week doesn't really matter, because we'll always be forgiven and comforted on Sunday morning.

Amazingly, one of the greatest illusions of the Christian faith is the church itself. There are millions of churches in the world – over 300,000 in the United States alone. But how many are actively growing? How many are preaching the gospel to those who've never heard it before? How many are actively serving and loving those in need? How many are making disciples, multiplying in number, and saving souls?

Church is so much more than Sunday.

I believe one of Satan's greatest victories is convincing believers that being a Christian equals attending a once-a-week event.

It's a devious attack on the Kingdom of God, and it happens under the guise of steeples, time slots, and tradition. The enemy is perfectly content letting us go through our Sunday morning rituals... as long as we don't actively live out our faith the rest of the week.

What terrifies the devil is not church on Sunday, but church on Monday.

When Church Becomes a Performance

This chapter is not meant to attack or forsake the church, but to help you experience the fullness of what God designed church to be.

Growing up, "church" meant a Sunday morning gathering comprised of all the right things to comfort Christians in their less-than-extraordinary walk with Christ. "Church" was synonymous with "routine." Dress pants and a dress shirt. Sunday school at 10:00 a.m., worship at 11:00, dinner at 1:00 p.m., then evening worship at 6:00, and snacks at 7:30. Everything about church revolved around a schedule.

As long as you didn't show up late, didn't drink, didn't swear, and didn't cheat on your spouse, you were considered a "good Christian." Those were the expectations. That was the pinnacle of redeeming grace.

Christianity was more about the things we didn't do rather than the things we did. Don't do this. Don't do that. The only thing we were expected to "do" was show up on Sunday.

What's wrong with this picture? Certainly, there are things the secular world does that Christians are commanded not to do. But there are also things Jesus commands us to do – things that the secular world has forsaken. For example, "Love your enemies" and "Go and make disciples of all the nations."

Too often, we have a pharisaical approach to what church is. The Pharisees were Jewish religious leaders who were fanatical about keeping traditions and rituals. When Jesus healed people on the Sabbath – the appointed day of rest – rather than rejoicing that a miracle had happened, the Pharisees criticized Jesus for healing on the Sabbath day. Their attitude was, "Couldn't that miracle have waited until tomorrow? Did this guy really need to be healed *today*? That wasn't on the schedule."

The Pharisees considered themselves to be righteous and holy because of their commitment to rituals and traditions. They even tithed 10% of their smallest garden herbs. Imagine picking every tenth leaf off of a tiny mint plant! But what did Jesus think of the Pharisees?

> *Then Jesus said to the crowds and to his disciples, "The teachers of religious law and the Pharisees are the official interpreters of the law of Moses. So practice and obey whatever they tell you, but don't follow their example. For they don't practice what they teach. They crush people with unbearable religious demands and never lift a finger to ease the burden. Everything they do is for show. On their arms they wear extra wide prayer boxes with Scripture verses inside, and they wear robes with extra long tassels. And they love to sit at the head table at banquets and in the seats of honor in the synagogues.... What sorrow awaits you teachers of religious law and you Pharisees. Hypocrites! For you are careful to tithe even the tiniest income from your herb gardens, but you ignore the more important aspects of the law—justice, mercy, and faith. You should tithe, yes, but do not neglect the more important things."*
>
> *Matthew 23:1-6, 23*

The Pharisees opposed Jesus because he took the focus off rituals, robes, and rules. The Pharisees loved to dress up in fancy religious clothing and pride themselves on how "holy" they looked. "Everything they do is for show." But Jesus took the focus off the outward appearance, and looked instead at the inward condition of the heart. Jesus spoke of personal relationships, supernatural empowerment, and being worldchangers moved by a contagious love. Jesus declared a new kind of Kingdom where it's not the ones wearing priestly robes who are holy, but forgiven sinners magnifying a holy God through an active faith.

We need to stop thinking like the Pharisees, and start thinking like Jesus.

Has "church" for you become nothing more than a weekly tradition?

Is church about looking nice on the outside, or is it about changing lives on the inside?

What is the Church?

The word "church" in the New Testament is the Greek word e*kklesia*, which means "an assembly" or "called-out ones." Contrary to popular belief, "church" is not a building. It's not Sunday morning, a sermon, or a tradition.

Church is you.

The church is the people and it has nothing to do with the steeple.

The greatest fallacy Christians have come to believe is that God is impressed with our nicely packaged Sunday Christianity. Sunday is great, but Jesus also cares about Monday through Saturday.

We are called to come together to worship God corporately and fellowship with other believers. But don't let your faith stop there.

> *Let us hold tightly without wavering to the hope we affirm, for God can be trusted to keep his promise. Let us think of ways to motivate one another to acts of love and good works. And let us not neglect our meeting together, as some people do, but encourage one another, especially now that the day of his return is drawing near.*
>
> *Hebrews 10:23-25*

Whether your local church worships on Sunday, Saturday, or another day of the week is not important. The date and time are not what matters – the worship is. We gather together, teach God's Word, build ministries, and elevate the great name of Jesus Christ.

We don't go to church – we *are* the church. Maybe once a week we set the model, but the model is only as good as our willingness to live it out every day.

Church begins on Monday.

Who is the Church?

The human body has many parts, but the many parts make up one whole body. So it is with the body of Christ. Some of us are Jews, some are Gentiles, some are slaves, and some are free. But we have all been baptized into one body by one Spirit, and we all share the same Spirit. Yes, the body has many different parts, not just one part. If the foot says, "I am not a part of the body because I am not a hand," that does not make it any less a part of the body. And if the ear says, "I am not part of the body because I am not an eye," would that make it any less a part of the body? If the whole body were an eye, how would you hear? Or if your whole body were an ear, how would you smell anything? But our bodies have many parts, and God has put each part just where he wants it. How strange a body would be if it had only one part! Yes, there are many parts, but only one body. The eye can never say to the hand, "I don't need you." The head can't say to the feet, "I don't need you." In fact, some parts of the body that seem weakest and least important are actually the most necessary. And the parts we regard as less honorable are those we clothe with the greatest care. So we carefully protect those parts that should not be seen, while the more honorable parts do not require this special care. So God has put the body together such that extra honor and care are given to those parts that have less dignity. This makes for harmony among the members, so that all the members care for each other. If one part suffers, all the parts suffer with it, and if one part is honored, all the parts are glad. All of you together are Christ's body, and each of you is a part of it.

1 Corinthians 12:12-27

The universal Church (capital "C") is made up of all believers in Jesus Christ around the world. Because Jesus ascended into heaven, He is no longer physically present in the world – and yet, He *is* present *through* us. Paul clearly declares that we, as Christians, are literally the body of Christ in the world today. Think about that for a moment. *You are His hands and His feet.* If you're a believer, His Spirit dwells within you, inspiring you to carry out His work in the world.

When Jesus walked the earth, He could only be in one place at a time. He was one man. Today, Jesus is even *more* present in the world than He was then, because He's working through millions of believers as they obediently follow His instructions. Today, His body is global and diverse, living and active, vast and powerful enough to change the world.

The body of Christ is made up of believers from the mega-church in the big city, the home church on a country back road, the mission church in the Congo, the underground church meeting secretly to escape persecution, and everything in between. The Church is every believer, everywhere. The body of Christ is not defined by denominations, sects, titles, labels, styles, or traditions. It is a universal, unified body of believers walking in the glory of God, for the glory of God.

My childhood is scarred by memories of judgmental Christians who truly believed that they were the only ones going to Heaven. Lest we forget, God's grace is about His grace, not about our "goods." The body of Christ is made up of anyone who has embraced the truth that Christ's body was given for them as an eternal sacrifice for their sins.

All those who are born again are born into the body of Christ.

In John 17, Jesus prayed that His Church would be one in the same way that He and the Father are one. So why is there often more competition between Christian denominations than there is in the Superbowl playoffs?

"The eye can never say to the hand, 'I don't need you.' The head can't say to the feet, 'I don't need you.'" Each member of the body is vitally important. The members need to be actively working *together* to accomplish Christ's work. And yet, much of the body of Christ currently lies fractured in little pieces – thousands of different denominations, with churches constantly splitting over the pettiest of disagreements.

It's not meant to be this way!

With ten fingers, I can accomplish a difficult task. If I'm missing even one finger, I will struggle. If I'm missing several fingers, it may be almost impossible. Just as I need all ten fingers in order to work most effectively, so the body of Christ needs all its members to carry out the work of Christ most effectively. Whatever your role is in the body of Christ, *you matter.* You are needed. Your obedient, faithful service is not in vain.

The local church (lower case "c") is the assembling of local believers in a corporate setting. The local church is designed by God to be the authorized vehicle through which believers worship together and equip each other to spread the Gospel around the world.

Although we may give our local churches names such as New Hope Community Church or Open Door Baptist Church, and even construct buildings to serve as places of worship, it's important to remember that the local church exists wherever believers are gathered. The local church doesn't necessarily need to have a name. It could gather in a home, a theater, a warehouse, or a parking lot just as easily as a traditional church building. God isn't confined to four walls and a steeple.

There are literally millions of local churches in the world, and together they make up the one universal Church, which is the complete body of Christ.

There is a growing trend in Christianity today of doing faith "on your own" without any "organized religion." But we are simply not designed to do this walk of faith alone. It is so important for every believer to be plugged in to a local church. The local church is called to be like a lighthouse on a hill for the lost villages of the world to see, and that light shines brightest when we put all of our individual lights together. There is something powerful about believers gathering together that cannot happen any other way.

The local church is the recipient of our tithes and offerings used to build ministries, spread the Gospel, make disciples, send missionaries, and meet the needs of those hurting both in the church family and the surrounding community. The first local church in the New Testament is found in Acts 2.

> *Those who believed what Peter said were baptized and added to the church that day—about 3,000 in all. All the*

believers devoted themselves to the apostles' teaching, and to fellowship, and to sharing in meals (including the Lord's Supper), and to prayer. A deep sense of awe came over them all, and the apostles performed many miraculous signs and wonders. And all the believers met together in one place and shared everything they had. They sold their property and possessions and shared the money with those in need. They worshiped together at the Temple each day, met in homes for the Lord's Supper, and shared their meals with great joy and generosity all the while praising God and enjoying the goodwill of all the people. And each day the Lord added to their fellowship those who were being saved.

Acts 2:41-47

This early church met in the homes of local believers. They didn't even have their own church building, yet "each day the Lord added to their fellowship those who were being saved."

One of the defining characteristics of the Acts 2 church is that *it was all about Jesus*. This church was radically committed to Jesus Christ – giving up everything to carry out His work. As a result, this church grew rapidly, with "a deep sense of awe" as the Gospel was preached, the hungry were fed, and miracles were performed.

This should be our example.

The same kind of power and growth that we see in Acts 2 can and *should* happen in every local church today. But unfortunately, many churches are not growing at all.

One of the biggest problems is that the name, style, schedule, activities, and programs of a local church often become more important than the Lord Jesus Christ. We schedule events simply because "we do that every year," even when God wants to lead us in a different direction. We resist change, maintaining our own preferences while a lost world goes unreached. Church becomes less about Jesus, and more about "church as usual." If we're not careful, church can be more about ownership than about borrowship.

If what we're doing isn't completely about Jesus, it's completely about us.

In the Book of Revelation, Jesus wrote seven letters to seven local churches. These letters contain powerful warnings relevant for local churches today. Jesus said:

> *"I know all the things you do, that you are neither hot nor cold. I wish that you were one or the other! But since you are like lukewarm water, neither hot nor cold, I will spit you out of my mouth! You say, 'I am rich. I have everything I want. I don't need a thing!' And you don't realize that you are wretched and miserable and poor and blind and naked. So I advise you to buy gold from me—gold that has been purified by fire. Then you will be rich. Also buy white garments from me so you will not be shamed by your nakedness, and ointment for your eyes so you will be able to see. I correct and discipline everyone I love. So be diligent and turn from your indifference."*
>
> Revelation 3:15-19

"Turn from your indifference." Is there a fire burning within you for your Savior? Are you passionate about seeing your local church grow and reach the lost? Or are you indifferent – content with church as usual?

Why Does the Church Do What it Does?

> *"Am I a God who is only close at hand?" says the LORD. "No, I am far away at the same time. Can anyone hide from me in a secret place? Am I not everywhere in all the heavens and earth?" says the LORD.*
>
> Jeremiah 23:23-24

The truest form of worship is **giving everything, to reach everyone** for a God who is **everywhere**. This is why the church does what it does.

God doesn't dwell only in your church building. Don't sell your daily encounter with God short by believing that the only place you can feel His presence is in your pew or kneeling before the altar on Sunday. Don't think He's only interested in meeting with you one day a week.

We serve an Everywhere God who calls us to be an Everyday Church.

The prophet Isaiah had a vision of the throne room of God. The glory of God's presence was so overwhelming that Isaiah never even got his eyes past God's robe, which filled the room. God's holiness was so powerful that Isaiah was grieved at the thought of his own sin. His encounter with the Almighty is backed by this anthem in Isaiah 6:2-4.

> *Attending him were mighty seraphim, each having six wings. With two wings they covered their faces, with two they covered their feet, and with two they flew. They were calling out to each other,* **"Holy, holy, holy is the LORD of Heaven's Armies! The whole earth is filled with his glory!"** *Their voices shook the Temple to its foundations, and the entire building was filled with smoke.*

The Hebrew word for "glory" here is *kabod*, which literally means "weight." It comes from the root word *kabed*, meaning "heavy with numerous riches." The anthem of the throne room of God was, "The earth is filled with the heavy weight of God's numerous riches" (my paraphrase). God's matchless presence is everywhere. Every step you take, God is there. He was there before and will be there after.

It's crazy to think that we try to put God inside a box.

What does it look like to have a daily relationship with a God who is everywhere? Consider the Garden of Eden. Adam and Eve lived in the absolute fullness of God's presence. There were no rituals. There were no traditions. There were no Sunday services. There was no religion. There was just God and humanity, living together in perfect harmony.

In your car, house, cubicle, locker room, classroom, or jail cell – *God is there!* Dwelling both in and around you, He is jealous for you to experience His glory and share it with the world (Exodus 34:14).

The Church is Blueprinted to live in His glory and share His glory. There is both a vertical and a horizontal dimension. We reach *up* to experience God, and we reach *out* to touch others with His love. This brings Him glory.

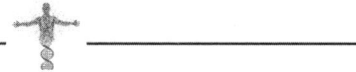

How Does the Church Do What it Does?

Christ is also the head of the church, which is his body. He is the beginning, supreme over all who rise from the dead. So he is first in everything.

Colossians 1:18

The local church is the assembling of the body of Christ in specific locations for the purpose of serving others, teaching God's Word, and worshiping Him. The shape of the local church is clearly defined in God's Blueprint.

If the local church is not properly structured, our experience of it will be unsuccessful and even detrimental.

The local church has a precise structure articulated by the Architect for optimum growth. Therefore, following His design is vitally important.

According to barna.org, a national church poll and research organization, between 3,500 and 4,000 local churches close their doors each year.

Local churches lose an estimated 2,700,000 people each year to secularism and moral relativism (the idea that morality is just a matter of personal opinion and nothing is really right or wrong.)

How is it possible that the most powerful movement ordained by God – the local church that offers the single greatest message of hope ever told – loses people to disappointing pipe dreams and temporary promises?

The shape is wrong.

Most people see church like this:

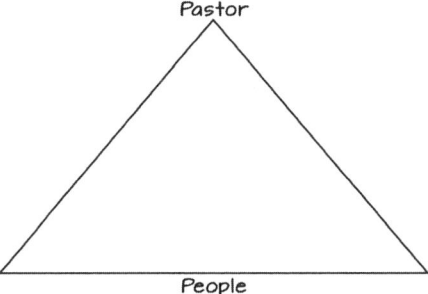

When a church is shaped like this, the pastor is the leader and focal point of everything. He is supposedly the closest to God, and he alone delivers God's Word to everyone else. The pastor has the ultimate authority and he can take the church in whatever direction he chooses.

You might think, "As long as you have a good pastor, what's wrong with that?" The first thing wrong is that it's sideline-enabling. The pastor runs the show, and the congregation sits on the sidelines. They come every Sunday to be instructed and encouraged by the pastor, but they never do their own study, encourage each other, or make their own disciples. The pastor may be working hard, but no one else is working. Like a muscle, what isn't used gets weak.

But there's another problem with this model that is even more deceiving. Although on the outside it may look like the pastor is enjoying life on the top, on the inside this structure ends up being more like this:

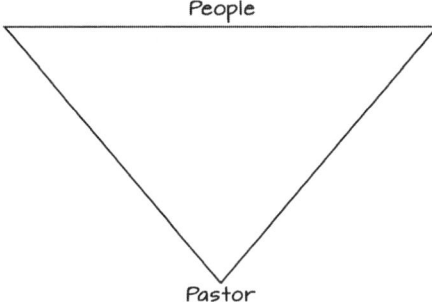

No pastor can bear the weight of the world upon his shoulders alone. Pastors are human too. A pastor simply cannot maintain the work of

The BLUEPRiNT | 195

running a local church, seeking God's will, studying God's Word, teaching every week, counseling people, and meeting the needs of the church family, all while simultaneously trying to be a husband and father, and maintain sanity on the homefront. If the entire church depends on the pastor, eventually the responsibility becomes too much for him, and he burns out.

New people visit the church and the pastor connects with them and they feel welcome. But others are resistant to change and want to maintain their same level of connection to the pastor. Over time the pastor can't juggle the demands of being all things to all people, and some people end up feeling slighted, and leave. It's a vicious cycle of "meet and greets" that ends in "empty seats." This shape is a recipe for discouragement. The body severs itself and the doors – held in place by a stubborn few who refuse to change – won't open to newcomers. Don't fuel this vehicle. The shape must change. Cars roll on circles, not triangles.

As a pastor, it took me six years of struggling, battling, and overexerting myself to understand that this triangular structure of church hierarchy simply doesn't work. It's all about the pastor, and not about Jesus. It has no shape of growth or glory. I think one of the biggest mistakes that pastors make is falling into the trap of this kind of church structure. We think we can do it all by ourselves, but we can't, and God doesn't ask us to!

The biblical model for the local church is actually more like this:

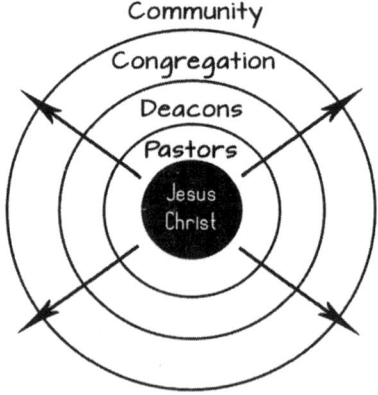

Now *this* is the shape of growth!

The Core: If growth is the target, Jesus Christ must be the bullseye. As it is in the home, Christ is the cornerstone of the church also. The focus, work, direction, and motivation of the church must be centered on Jesus Christ alone. Have you ever walked into church and immediately felt the presence of the Lord? His presence should fill the church. The more obedient we are to Jesus Christ, the deeper our experience of Him becomes. As a church remains obedient to Christ, His inner circle expands larger and larger. The expansion of Christ is not only strengthening, but intoxicating. The more Christ is exalted, the more we experience His abundant riches. But be warned: The more that the pastor or any other person is exalted, the less Christ is exalted.

$$\text{All of me} = \text{None of Christ}$$

$$\text{Less of me} = \text{More of Christ}$$

$$\text{None of me} = \text{All of Christ}$$

Pastors/Elders: Pastors serve a vitally important role in the local church, but not for their own glory. Pastors are called to shepherd the flock for the glory of the Lord. Peter wrote in 1 Peter 5:2,

> *Care for the flock that God has entrusted to you. Watch over it willingly, not grudgingly—not for what you will get out of it, but because you are eager to serve God.*

Every good shepherd provides three things for his sheep: direction, food, and care. Pastors are called to lead by establishing a structure that will provide these three growth-defining components to the local church.

Direction: The direction or vision that the Lord gives a pastor for the church is important, but it's a pastor's ability to lead that will determine whether or not the vision will come to fruition. Once again, humility is key. The pastor must remember he can't do it on his own. The vision is for the whole church to carry out, not just the pastor.

> *Where there is no vision, the people perish: but he that keepeth the law, happy is he.*
>
> Proverbs 29:18 KJV

The church must be built by believers who are actively involved. No matter how great the pastor's vision, it will never become reality without the involvement of the entire local church. In order for people to catch the vision, they must be active, fed, and cared for. The greater the leading, feeding, and caring, the greater the growth.

Great leaders lead people to become great leaders. A pastor must be committed to growth, not personal gain.

Feeding: My youngest son, Karter, has a favorite dinnertime saying: "I don't yike (like) it." No matter what the food, he always assumes he won't like it. My wife is unaffected by Karter's mindset. She decides what to cook, and that's what's served. Nine times out of ten, Karter discovers that what he thought he wouldn't "yike" he actually "yikes!"

There is a common misconception that preaching a watered-down gospel will draw more people in the doors. In reality, we're designed with a supernatural hunger for truth that can only be satisfied by the convicting, uplifting, and exciting power of God's Word. Although truth is sometimes difficult to hear, God's Word builds up the local church. A pastor must prayerfully feed the flock the spiritual food God provides through the leading of the Holy Spirit.

> *When I am with those who are weak, I share their weakness, for I want to bring the weak to Christ. Yes, I try to find common ground with everyone, doing everything I can to save some. I do everything to spread the Good News and share in its blessings.*
>
> *1 Corinthians 9:22-23*

In these verses, Paul passionately declares his desire to reach the lost by any means necessary. When the Word of God is preached with love and compassion, it breaks down barriers and penetrates the hearts of all who hear. Pastors are called to creatively present and teach God's Word in a way that is culturally relevant. Although the methods of teaching change over time, the Message never changes. Paul says in 2 Timothy 4:2,

> *Preach the word of God. Be prepared, whether the time is favorable or not. Patiently correct, rebuke, and encourage your people with good teaching.*

Great teachers require great students. The greatest message can be preached, but if the hearts of the people are not prepared to receive it, it will have no impact. Jesus said in Matthew 13:3-9,

> *"Listen! A farmer went out to plant some seeds. As he scattered them across his field, some seeds fell on a footpath, and the birds came and ate them. Other seeds fell on shallow soil with underlying rock. The seeds sprouted quickly because the soil was shallow. But the plants soon wilted under the hot sun, and since they didn't have deep roots, they died. Other seeds fell among thorns that grew up and choked out the tender plants. Still other seeds fell on fertile soil, and they produced a crop that was thirty, sixty, and even a hundred times as much as had been planted! Anyone with ears to hear should listen and understand."*

In most local churches, a pastor teaches one day each week. But you must be in God's Word every day with a heart of fertile soil, actively applying what you learn. The more you apply what you learn, the more you hunger to learn more, and the more fertile your soil becomes. This is the key for leadership development in the local church.

Care: A pastor is called to "care for the flock" by building relationships with the people. But a pastor is only one person. To effectively care for a growing community, a pastor must raise up deacons to share this responsibility.

Deacons: Like shepherds protecting their sheep from ravenous wolves, pastors must care for the community of believers. But pastors are not called to bear this burden alone. A pastor's ability to raise up leadership is vitally important to the health of the local church. Acts 6:1-7 reads:

> *But as the believers rapidly multiplied, there were rumblings of discontent. The Greek-speaking believers complained about the Hebrew-speaking believers, saying that their widows were being discriminated against in the daily distribution of food. So the Twelve called a meeting of all the believers. They said, "We apostles should spend our time teaching the word of God, not running a food program. And so, brothers, select seven men who are well*

respected and are full of the Spirit and wisdom. We will give them this responsibility. Then we apostles can spend our time in prayer and teaching the word." Everyone liked this idea, and they chose the following: Stephen (a man full of faith and the Holy Spirit), Philip, Procorus, Nicanor, Timon, Parmenas, and Nicolas of Antioch (an earlier convert to the Jewish faith). These seven were presented to the apostles, who prayed for them as they laid their hands on them. So God's message continued to spread. The number of believers greatly increased in Jerusalem, and many of the Jewish priests were converted, too.

Whether your church uses the word "deacon" is not important. What matters is that the local church has additional leadership serving the people as an extension of the pastor, to care for the people and handle their needs. Increase Christ. Increase leadership. Increase care. This is the shape of a healthy church Blueprinted for maximum growth.

The Home: The home is the glue of the local church. Pastors, elders, and deacons are all called to have biblical homes in order to qualify for those responsibilities (1 Timothy 3:1-13). Families anchored in the principles of God's Word expand the growing power of the local church.

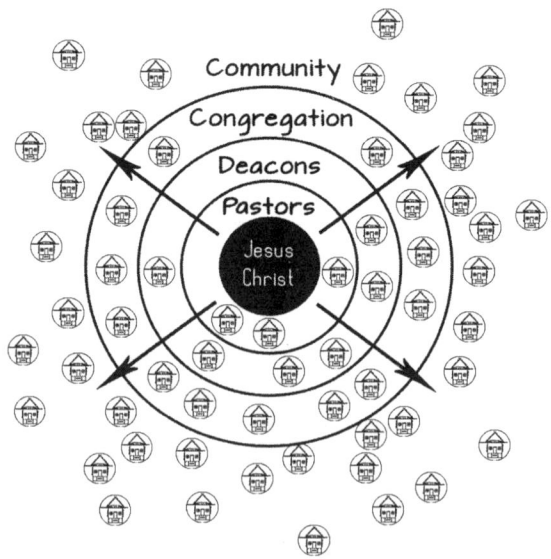

A family that qualifies is a family that quantifies.

Is your family part of a local church? Is your family actively serving?

The desire of your heart should be to grow and serve at your greatest capacity. Jesus Christ has given you full authority to change the world. Leaders are grown from the home through the church. Are you on the bench rooting for your pastor while your church struggles to grow?

Church is not a spectator sport.

It's time to get up and get going, both at home and at church. Your home is more powerful and more important than you realize.

What's My Role in the Church?

Look at the obvious facts. Those who say they belong to Christ must recognize that we belong to Christ as much as they do. I may seem to be boasting too much about the authority given to us by the Lord. But our authority builds you up; it doesn't tear you down. So I will not be ashamed of using my authority.

I'm not trying to frighten you by my letters. For some say, "Paul's letters are demanding and forceful, but in person he is weak, and his speeches are worthless!" Those people should realize that our actions when we arrive in person will be as forceful as what we say in our letters from far away.

Oh, don't worry; we wouldn't dare say that we are as wonderful as these other men who tell you how important they are! But they are only comparing themselves with each other, using themselves as the standard of measurement. How ignorant!

We will not boast about things done outside our area of authority. We will boast only about what has happened within the boundaries of the work God has given us, which includes our working with you. We are not reaching beyond these boundaries when we claim authority over you, as if we had never visited you. For we were the first to travel all the way to Corinth with the Good News of Christ.

Nor do we boast and claim credit for the work someone else has done. Instead, we hope that your faith will grow so that the boundaries of our work among you will be extended. Then we will be able to go and preach the Good News in other places far beyond you, where no one else is working. Then there will be no question of our boasting about work done in someone else's territory. As the Scriptures say, "If you want to boast, boast only about the Lord."

When people commend themselves, it doesn't count for much. The important thing is for the Lord to commend them.

2 Corinthians 10:7-18

You are a gifted member of the body of Christ. You are not just a believer, but an important part of the Church. Your life's mission is engulfed in the very real call to be all God has called you to be. Your role in the local church is purposefully authorized by the Lord Jesus Christ. This passage in 2 Corinthians records Paul's letter to the people who collectively formed the local church in Corinth. Paul's words start by addressing the idea that some people in the church felt like they were more valuable than others because of their "abilities." Paul wasn't a great speaker so some were attacking his writings because he couldn't back them up with eloquent words. Others felt they had greater authority because they were physically present in Corinth while Paul was not.

Paul points out some important truths concerning your role in the local church. Church is not a talent show or a place for men to be elevated above other people. If you receive praise for your abilities, humbly remember that you were bought with a price. God gave you those abilities to bring glory to Himself, not you. Maybe you serve in a less noticeable role such as that of a prayer warrior, nursery volunteer, or parking attendant. Even if you receive little praise for your work, rest assured that the Lord is multiplying your efforts to make a difference in the world. Your work is important and your faithfulness is not in vain.

When we planted Love City Fellowship in Gloversville, New York, people asked me, "Why are you planting a church there when there are already other churches in the area?" But I knew the Lord had called us to plant this church. His plan for redemption should never be questioned. It makes no difference whether there is one local church in an area or a hundred, as long as they are all actively doing the Lord's work. The only reason why someone would be bitter about a healthy church growing in "their area" is because their church is about the sign by the road and not the Savior.

Paul wrote that he wouldn't boast about being successful in areas where others are already preaching, as if he were a better preacher. It really didn't matter to him whose area belonged to whom. He just wanted to see the Gospel move! He wrote, *"If you want to boast, boast only about the Lord."* The enemy will use feelings of jealousy and ownership to separate the body of Christ and divide the Church. Don't fall victim to this lie.

Go where the Lord leads you to go. It doesn't matter who is there, or what they will think of you. Go with confidence in Christ.

Church should be all about action.

If your local church is the same size today as it was a year ago, there's something wrong.

If your church isn't making an impact on the surrounding community, there's something wrong.

If your church isn't equipping people to go out and reach the lost, there's something wrong.

I'm not sure what it is about church that sucks people into this mindset that it's better to be a spectator than an active player. When I was in high school, the last thing I wanted to do during a basketball game was warm the bench. *I wanted to be in the game.* I wanted to contribute something to the team. I wanted to be part of the victory.

Christians everywhere need to wake up and realize that merely being a churchgoer is not the same as being a faithful disciple of Jesus Christ.

Which are you?

There are three dangerous things I hear people say when it comes to being active in their faith through the local church:

"I don't feel like I'm connecting." The reason you don't feel like you're connecting at your local church is *because* you are not connecting! The church of Acts 2 was flooded by fellowship. They didn't just have a weekly meeting. They enjoyed life together day in and day out. They ate together. They prayed together. They remembered the Lord together through Communion. *They connected.* You'll never experience the warmth of relationships unless you begin to invest in them. It's not the pastor's job to connect you with the believers around you. You are responsible for investing effort into building relationships with your church family.

Here are a few ideas to get started: Join a small group Bible study. Start a small group Bible study. Start a men's breakfast or women's ministry. Start a fitness group. Whether you join a community already in existence, or you start your own, you won't feel like you're connecting *until you connect.* It's that simple.

> *Two people are better off than one, for they can help each other succeed. If one person falls, the other can reach out and help. But someone who falls alone is in real trouble. Likewise, two people lying close together can keep each other warm. But how can one be warm alone? A person standing alone can be attacked and defeated, but two can stand back-to-back and conquer. Three are even better, for a triple-braided cord is not easily broken.*
>
> *Ecclesiastes 4:9-12*

"I don't feel like I'm called." This one definitely makes the list of "Top 10 Things Christians Say... That Are Dumb." My uncle Wes tells a story of a conversation he had with one of his employees. This employee was one of those people who talks an incredible game, but shows almost no actual results. Whenever he was asked a question, he would give long answers with sophisticated words and seemingly profound thoughts. By the time he finished an answer, you'd forgotten what the question was. One day there was a problem with a machine and production was halted. My uncle went in and said, "What's wrong with the machine?" The employee responded with five minutes of babble. When he finally finished talking, my uncle said:

"Your actions are so loud that I can't hear what you're saying."

If you're a believer, you're called. Period. You can try to talk your way out of it, but you can't change the fact that God is calling you to *do something*. Maybe you don't know yet what area of ministry God wants you to serve in. In the meantime, start serving somewhere! If you wait for God to reveal His entire plan for your life, you'll be waiting your whole life. He reveals it to us piece-by-piece. We have to be faithful with the first step before He can give us the second step. It's a process. In his book *Greater*, Senior Pastor Steven Furtick of Elevation Church writes:

"Stop trying to audition for the role God has already given you."

A stagnant faith is motionless. It resists change. It doesn't want to see revival because it's content with business as usual. It has no desire to grow. It doesn't really care if the lost are reached. If your faith is stagnant, you are lukewarm, and in danger of Jesus spitting you out of His mouth (Revelation 3:16). A stagnant faith is extremely dangerous, because it isn't really faith at all.

An active faith is *driven*. It has momentum. It moves you to move people. It makes it impossible to sit still for too long. An active faith is restless for revival and desperate for change. It yearns for growth. An active faith lives to reach the lost. If your faith is active, you're not lukewarm – you're on fire.

> *What good is it, dear brothers and sisters, if you say you have faith but don't show it by your actions? Can that kind of faith save anyone? Suppose you see a brother or sister who has no food or clothing, and you say, "Goodbye and have a good day; stay warm and eat well"—but then you don't give that person any food or clothing. What good does that do? So you see, faith by itself isn't enough. Unless it produces good deeds, it is dead and*

> *useless. Now someone may argue, "Some people have faith; others have good deeds." But I say, "How can you show me your faith if you don't have good deeds? I will show you my faith by my good deeds." You say you have faith, for you believe that there is one God. Good for you! Even the demons believe this, and they tremble in terror. How foolish! Can't you see that faith without good deeds is useless?*
>
> *James 2:14-20*

James isn't saying we're saved by our good deeds, but that genuine faith always produces good deeds. If your faith isn't moving you to make changes in your life, what's the point? Faith that doesn't transform us isn't real faith at all – it's dead.

I'm especially struck by this: *"'Some people have faith; others have good deeds.' But I say, 'How can you show me your faith if you don't have good deeds?'"*

Have you ever heard something like this? "Some people are called to be missionaries, but others are simply called to have faith." "Some people are called to be involved in serving, but others just have faith." "Preaching and making disciples is the pastor's job, my job is simply to believe in God." This kind of thinking is extremely dangerous. The reality is that real faith always produces action. Faith without action is dead.

There is no such thing as "believing" without doing anything. If you're a believer, *you're active!*

"Smaller churches are more intimate." Intimacy in a church can be a great cover for laziness. It can cause stagnant comfort. Laziness says, "Let's just stay like this, just the few of us. We don't want to get too big and lose what we have." This attitude is the opposite of love. Love says, "We need to share this gift with everyone and build what God has given us so all that Jesus suffered for doesn't go to waste." Intimacy can't be lost by expanding love. Intimacy is maximized by expanding love. Love always wins. 1 Corinthians 13:1-3 says this about love:

> *If I could speak all the languages of earth and of angels, but didn't love others, I would only be a noisy gong or a*

> *clanging cymbal. If I had the gift of prophecy, and if I understood all of God's secret plans and possessed all knowledge, and if I had such faith that I could move mountains, but didn't love others, I would be nothing. If I gave everything I have to the poor and even sacrificed my body, I could boast about it; but if I didn't love others, I would have gained nothing.*

It doesn't matter how much you know about the Bible. It doesn't matter how faithful you are in your tithing. It doesn't even matter if you volunteer for the food pantry every week. If you don't have love – everything you do is in vain.

If you love the lost, you won't be satisfied with your local church staying the same size. Love fuels growth! And growth fuels intimacy. True intimacy is found in the overwhelming presence of the Holy Spirit in every believer. Our desire should be to share His presence without hesitation.

If we go to church on Sunday but don't give God a second thought Monday through Saturday, do we really love Him?

The enemy would love for our faith to become nothing more than a scheduled event – another entry on the calendar. We gather every Sunday for comfort and encouragement, hoping to feel that emotional "high." We become more like leeches than lovers. Everything has to be perfect for us to leave feeling spiritually "full." That's not love, it's lust – lust for the effects of God rather than the love of affecting others for God.

Do you love God enough to get off the bench and get busy doing His will?

Do you love God enough to stop merely going to church, and start *being* the Church? Do you love God enough to share Him with others?

If you aren't reaching the lost with the Gospel message, you aren't loving God and others as the Blueprint empowers you to love.

> *"For God loved the world so much that he gave his one and only Son, so that everyone who believes in him will not perish but have eternal life."*
>
> John 3:16

QUESTIONS. ADDITIONAL STUDY. APPLICATION.

Thoughts from Chapter 8: The Not-So-Sunday Church

The universal Church is made up of every believer everywhere. The local church is made of believers who come together in communities around the world. The church is not a building, a tradition, or a denomination. The church is people. You don't go to church. You *are* the church. God has given the local church a Blueprint for a structure that promotes growth and care. You are called to connect with your church family. You are called to be active in your faith, using your abilities to serve. True intimacy is found when the love of Christ is shared with the masses. Love always wins!

Questions to Consider

How would answer this question, "What is church?"

How do Christ's words against the Pharisees change the way you view church?

Is your local church structured according to the Blueprint? If not, how could it be improved?

Is your home part of the "glue" that holds the local church together?

Is your faith active? What are some ways you are fulfilling your role in the body of Christ through your local church?

Are you connecting and building relationships with others at your local church? If not, what are some ways you can get connected?

Do you feel like you're called? Have you identified what ministries God is calling you to serve in? If not, what would be a good way to start serving?

Do you think smaller churches are more intimate? If so, why? What are some things you can do to maintain intimacy as your church grows?

Additional Verses to Study / How Can i Apply This?

Five Aspects of Corporate Worship

- **Teaching:** Ephesians 4:11-16 and Matthew 7:15-23

- **Worship:** Psalm 150 and Psalm 95:1-7

- **Prayer:** 2 Chronicles 7:14-15 and James 5:13-20

- **Communion:** Luke 22:14-20 and 1 Corinthians 11:23-29

- **Unity:** John 17 and Romans 16:17-20

Building Blocks: Before i Move On...

☐ I am the Church.

☐ I am called.

☐ I am actively serving in my local church.

☐ I am intentionally building relationships with my church family.

☐ I am not content with church as usual. I am eager for growth.

Prayer

Heavenly Father, I praise You for Your faithfulness to my local church. Lord, I am hungry for revival and desperate for growth. Please inspire my pastors and church leadership to effectively structure my church according to Your Blueprint. Help me to serve with passion in the specific ministries You are calling me to. What an awesome privilege it is to literally be the body of Christ in the world today! Please inspire me, move me, and empower me to boldly go out and accomplish the work of Christ. Amen.

CHAPTER 9
THE GREAT COMMISSION

Jesus came and told his disciples, "I have been given all authority in heaven and on earth. Therefore, go and make disciples of all the nations, baptizing them in the name of the Father and the Son and the Holy Spirit. Teach these new disciples to obey all the commands I have given you. And be sure of this: I am with you always, even to the end of the age."

Matthew 28:18-20

In the single greatest transition of power in history, Jesus Christ placed the authority of Heaven in our hands and told us to go, baptize, and teach.

Everything we've covered in this book leads to one thing: **The Great Commission.**

The Blueprint is not complete until it's duplicated in the life of another.

Sixty-six books, 1,189 chapters, and 31,102 verses of Scripture all culminate with the Great Commission.

It's the change of one, by one, for the One – and repeat.

The Great Commission is not just for missionaries headed to the far corners of the globe. It's not just for the Apostles or the early Church. The Great Commission is for *every* disciple today, tomorrow, and until the end of the age.

Disciples make disciples, and those disciples make more disciples. The building of the Kingdom of God is driven by divine multiplication. This is the supernatural, universal call of every believer.

All of Heaven waits in anticipation as the body of Christ moves in a quest to multiply disciples. *Your life is purposed for discipleship.* Each breath you take is a breath given to you by God *for* His pursuit of others.

The Great Commission is literally the reason you are alive today.

Your relationship with the Savior of the world revolves around the people near you. He promises you the ultimate relationship with a Holy God and the supernatural byproduct of that awesome relationship is the salvation of others.

People are His passion. People are your purpose. Jesus said:

> *"Don't store up treasures here on earth, where moths eat them and rust destroys them, and where thieves break in and steal. Store your treasures in heaven, where moths and rust cannot destroy, and thieves do not break in and steal. Wherever your treasure is, there the desires of your heart will also be."*
>
> *Matthew 6:19-21*

This passage of Scripture grips and convicts my life. We are called to store up treasures in Heaven. We are called by Jesus Christ to make Heavenly deposits here on earth. How is that possible? First, we know that God's glory is a weight of riches that passes all understanding. God is beyond all form of earthly wealth and materialism.

How do we, as gravity-pulled people, invest in a Heavenly treasury? By investing in the only thing in this world with eternal value: **people**.

"Don't store up treasures on earth."

Jesus didn't say "You probably shouldn't" or "It would really be great if you didn't."

He said "don't."

Our lives can't be consumed by things that won't make it past the grave.

Are you raising your children in the faith? Are you telling your friends what God has done for you? You may be the only reflection of Jesus Christ they ever see.

One day, Heaven will reveal itself in a glorious fashion and this world's pursuits and temporary riches will pale in comparison. Where are you storing your treasures? When was the last time you made a Heavenly deposit?

Your ability to be a disciple maker can be found in this equation:

Your Means x Your Motive = Your Ability to Multiply

Take what you have and multiply it by your heart for others – this is your multiplying power. If you refuse to surrender your means, the equation is busted. If giving is all you want to do, but you have no passion to share Jesus, the formula doesn't work. God is a God of multiplication.

Go. Baptize. Teach. This is the Great Commission, and it was given to every believer by the Lord Jesus Christ – the Author in full AUTHORity.

Go: Me And My Jesus Swagger

> <u>Swagger</u>: *"How one presents himself or herself to the world. Swagger is shown in how one handles a situation. Swagger is also shown in one's walk."*

"How one presents himself or herself to the world." Swagger. It's the confidence of knowing who you are and not being afraid to show it.

Why is it that non-Christians walk around with a confidence that many Christians – ambassadors of the Lord of the universe – fail to have?

It's time to get some swagger.

> *"The Son of Man, on the other hand, feasts and drinks, and you say, 'He's a glutton and a drunkard, and a friend of tax collectors and other sinners!' But wisdom is shown to be right by its results."*
>
> Matthew 11:19

The "religious" people hated the fact that Jesus was popular. The Bible certainly doesn't say that He was a glutton or a drunkard – Jesus was sinless. But these were the rumors spread by so-called "righteous" people because Jesus was loved by those they wanted nothing to do with.

Jesus was a friend to sinners. He was sinless, yet sinners liked him. Sinners wanted to be around him. Weird.

I'm currently trying to disciple a young man in our community. He looks straight-up "gangster" from all cultural appearances. With diamonds in the ears, extra long 2-XL t-shirts, and a Mercedes-Benz with 20" chrome rims, hip-hop bumpin' – he's got all the bling and he rolls with swagger. I met him on the basketball court and made an instant friendship. Why?

The secular world might never understand why I'd make friends with this person. I mean, I'm a white guy (I mean really white) who pastors a church and drives a minivan. We live on different planets, but we have one thing in common: basketball.

I hit the court in my long shorts and J's (Jordans), ready to ball with the boys. I've earned their respect by putting it all on the floor and being a baller. Because of the basketball skills God blessed me with, I'm part of a community I would otherwise have nothing in common with. *I'm determined to use that connection for God's glory.*

Maybe by the time you read this, one of my rides in his Benz will result in a true surrender to Jesus Christ.

Go, and make disciples of all nations.

The command to "go" should be the foundation for everything we do. We tend to think that "making disciples of all nations" means sending missionaries overseas. That's just one part of it. "All nations" also includes your next-door neighbor, the people you see every day at work, and the guys you go golfing or fishing with.

"All nations" means *everyone*.

God gave you unique skills and relationships that connect you with specific people. Are you using those connections to build His Kingdom?

If you don't share the Gospel with the people in your life… who will?

Christians who walk around with their noses in the air – wrapped in righteous robes and keeping the lost at arm's length – aren't proud of their Jesus, they're afraid to share their Jesus. They put on the swagger of self-righteousness to cover up their lack of "Jesus swagger" – the confidence to openly display their faith in Christ without being ashamed to share it.

Our lives should be all about making disciples of all nations, all the time. That doesn't mean we can't enjoy the many activities and entertainment this world has to offer – like playing basketball, for example. But use those things as vehicles to build relationships and reach the lost. It's one thing to simply play basketball. It's another to shine as the light of the world on the court, being the hands and feet of Jesus as you score buckets for God's Kingdom. God wants to raise you up to shine as a light in your circle of influence.

Stop being embarrassed about your faith. Start declaring it with confidence. Only *you* can reach *your* circle of influence. Be yourself. Be light. Be the friend of sinners. Be contagious.

"Swagger is shown in how one handles a situation." Sometimes you just have to shut up and get up. No one ever said this Christian walk would be easy. I realize there are times when you want to speak your mind and tell someone like it is, but Jesus swagger is about handling situations as He would. The mouth can be your greatest tool or your greatest failure. Your tongue is more powerful than any other weapon you could equip yourself with. You'd better be careful what you speak. James 3:2-6 reads:

> *Indeed, we all make many mistakes. For if we could control our tongues, we would be perfect and could also control ourselves in every other way. We can make a large horse go wherever we want by means of a small bit in its mouth. And a small rudder makes a huge ship turn wherever the pilot chooses to go, even though the winds are strong. In the same way, the tongue is a small thing that makes grand speeches. But a tiny spark can set a great forest on fire. And the tongue is a flame of fire. It is a whole world of wickedness, corrupting your entire body. It can set your whole life on fire, for it is set on fire by hell itself.*

The words you speak reveal what's in your heart.

> *A good person produces good things from the treasury of a good heart, and an evil person produces evil things from the treasury of an evil heart. What you say flows from what is in your heart.*
>
> Luke 6:45

There is no greater example of a powerful tongue than Jesus Christ. Not once during the entire suffering of His crucifixion did He speak a harmful word to anyone. He was spit on, beaten, mocked, and nailed to a Cross, yet He endured it all silently. He said it all by saying nothing at all.

People around you will test you. They want to see if your faith is real. They'll try to make you violate your faith, just to prove you wrong, and it's easy to give in.

The Christian who screams words of anger at the guy who just did him wrong. The Christian who swears at the guy who cuts him off on the highway. The Christian who can't resist insulting the guy who just insulted him.

These are times when the Great Commission fails. One misspoken word can kill your witness.

There will always be that guy. There will always be that guy who mistreats you, cuts you off, angers you, mocks you. Stop taking it personally and start taking it faithfully. Control your tongue and preserve your witness. Remain in the forgiving love of Jesus. If you mess up, make it right.

Sometimes suffering is the way of the Savior.

> *Don't use foul or abusive language. Let everything you say be good and helpful, so that your words will be an encouragement to those who hear them.*
>
> Ephesians 4:29

"Swagger is also shown in one's walk." Being a disciple is a moment-by-moment commitment. In Jewish tradition, a disciple would follow his rabbi everywhere. It was considered a great honor to be literally covered in the dust of a rabbi from following him closely on the dirt roads and sitting at his feet as he taught.

The Mishnah is a collection of rabbinic thought compiled in the year 220 A.D. but based on much earlier oral tradition. The following quotation from the Mishnah (Pirkei Avot 1:4) is attributed to Yose ben Yoezer, a rabbi who lived about 200 years before Christ.

> *Let your house be a meeting-house for the wise; and powder yourself in the dust of their feet; and drink their words with thirstiness.*

Are you covered in the dust of the Savior? We're called to be dirty with devoted discipleship. Jesus told his disciples in Luke 9:3-5,

> *"Take nothing for your journey," he instructed them. "Don't take a walking stick, a traveler's bag, food, money, or even a change of clothes. Wherever you go, stay in the same house until you leave town. And if a town refuses to welcome you, **shake its dust from your feet** as you leave to show that you have abandoned those people to their fate."*

Jesus was telling his followers to be unaffected by those who rejected them. By shaking off the dust of those who rejected the truth, the disciples were saying, "Folks, you're walking down a path we can't follow."

Is your walk covering you with the dust of Jesus Christ or the dirt of this world?

To have real Jesus swagger, we must walk as He walked.

It's a walk of compassion and selflessness. It's a walk of giving before receiving. It's a walk of loving enemies and being peacemakers. It's a walk of being different enough to make a lost world searching for hope stop and take notice.

It's a walk that will change the world.

The Blueprint for "Go" starts with radical acts of kindness that ignite a desire for Christ in the hearts of those hungry for lifechange.

One day Jesus will return to rule as King over all the earth. The dead will rise and be judged before His throne. He tells us what will happen:

> *"Then the King will say to those on his right, 'Come, you who are blessed by my Father, inherit the Kingdom prepared for you from the creation of the world. For I was hungry, and you fed me. I was thirsty, and you gave me a drink. I was a stranger, and you invited me into your home. I was naked, and you gave me clothing. I was sick, and you cared for me. I was in prison, and you visited me.' Then these righteous ones will reply, 'Lord, when did we ever see you hungry and feed you? Or thirsty and give you something to drink? Or a stranger and show you hospitality? Or naked and give you clothing? When did we ever see you sick or in prison and visit you?' And the King will say, 'I tell you the truth, when you did it to one of the least of these my brothers and sisters, you were doing it to me!'"*
>
> Matthew 25:34-40

Shoveling your neighbor's driveway, paying for someone's coffee at Dunkin' Donuts, visiting someone in the hospital, writing a note of encouragement, holding a door, dropping off cookies – these are examples of "the little things." Most people think the little things don't matter. But the little things are everything. The little things can change someone's eternal destiny. Whatever we do to "the least of these" we are doing to Jesus. So, the next time you shovel your neighbor's driveway, consider this: *You are shoveling Jesus' driveway.*

It's easy to think that only "big" acts of service matter. But every "big" act of service is made up of a whole bunch of smaller acts of service. You can't do the big things if you're not willing to do the little things.

If you're not faithful in the little things, you're not faithful in anything (Luke 16:10).

Every act of kindness – no matter how small – changes the course of history.

Walking with the Lord is a day-by-day, moment-by-moment, little-thing-by-little-thing walk.

Be faithful in your walk. Be unwavering in your walk. Share your walk.

Let your daily walk be a dusty one. Walk with swagger.

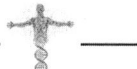

Everyone, Everywhere

Jesus told us to make disciples of all nations. "All" means everyone, everywhere, no exceptions. One of the saddest assumptions you can make about someone is that they are unreachable – that "even if I shared my faith with them, there's no way they would accept Christ."

We're talking about a person Jesus loved enough to die for. Can you really *assume* they're unreachable?

Sadly, it's human nature to make judgments about people. We see people, we assume we know their "type," and we draw conclusions about them before we ever get to know them.

You're at the local deli, waiting in line to order some subs. You've never seen the guy in front of you before, but you think you know his "type." He's that guy with the camouflage and hunting boots. Yeah, that guy. He probably drives a Ford F350 pickup truck with double stacks blowing diesel smoke 20 feet in the air. Oh, you definitely know the type. He must be the guy with Brad Paisley blaring and a half-empty Budweiser in the cupholder; maybe even a Confederate flag on the bumper. He's bound to have a shotgun hanging in the back window and a buck knife in the glove box. Undoubtedly, he has a dead deer hanging in his garage and the blood is dripping all over the floor. There's no way *that guy* wants to hear about Jesus!

NO.

You do NOT know him!

Do NOT assume you know!

That kind of thinking is stupid for two reasons. First of all, you know *nothing* about this guy. For all you know, he could be a Wall Street executive who decided to try on some camo for his first day hunting.

Secondly, even if you're right and the guy *does* drive a Ford F350 with a shotgun in the back and a dead deer in the garage... so what? Why does that mean he doesn't want Jesus? It's dumb to think that, because I know plenty of people just like that who *love* Jesus!

The devil loves to instill fear and intimidation in us – whatever it takes to keep us from reaching out to others. Never assume that anyone is too different or too intimidating to want Jesus. Odds are those people *do* want Jesus, but no one has had the boldness to share Him with them.

"All nations" is everyone, everywhere – from India to Indianapolis.

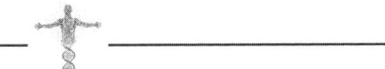

Baptize: 360° of Change

Jesus came and told his disciples, "I have been given all authority in heaven and on earth. Therefore, go and make disciples of all the nations, baptizing them in the name of the Father and the Son and the Holy Spirit. Teach these new disciples to obey all the commands I have given you. And be sure of this: I am with you always, even to the end of the age."

Matthew 28:18-20

The command to "go and make disciples of all the nations" is immediately followed by the command to baptize.

Baptism is an essential part of the Great Commission. It is equally as important as the command to "go." Baptism is the Blueprinted confirmation of every believer's faith in Jesus Christ. Obedience in baptism is the first big step we're called to take after Salvation. Baptism is clearly commanded in Scripture, and it serves an essential role in discipleship.

> *Those who believed what Peter said were baptized and added to the church that day—about 3,000 in all.*
>
> *Acts 2:41*

Filled with the Holy Spirit, Peter stepped in front of thousands of people and preached the Gospel message. Now let's be clear, this was no warm and fuzzy event. This is not some Sunday school story with cute little cartoony illustrations. This is a moment that changed history.

Jesus Christ had just turned the world upside down with miracles, counter-cultural teaching, and a death and resurrection that shook the foundations of the universe. Total darkness had fallen over the land the moment Jesus died. The earth quaked, the Temple veil broke in two, graves opened, and the dead walked. Just three days later, Jesus Christ rose from the dead, appearing first to the women at the tomb, then the disciples, and then hundreds of witnesses, before finally giving the Great Commission and ascending into heaven.

These events had taken place just several weeks prior to Peter's great sermon. And yet the name of Jesus had already spread like wildfire across the land. When Peter stood up to speak at Pentecost, this simple fisherman was thrust into the spotlight of a worldchanging movement, called in that pivotal moment to preach a message of life, countercultural love, and limitless discipleship.

As the Holy Spirit was poured out at Pentecost, the disciples received the miraculous ability to speak in other languages. Some people were critical of the message and accused the disciples of being drunk (Acts 2:13). Imagine how intimidating it must have been for Peter to preach the Gospel before that crowd of skeptics and critics, some of whom were even responsible for crucifying Jesus (Acts 2:36). This is the same Peter who, less than two months earlier, denied Jesus three times because he was too embarrassed to admit he was a disciple (Luke 22:54-62).

Yet the Holy Spirit did something amazing that day, empowering Peter to preach with boldness. As Peter spoke, the Spirit moved upon the souls of those searching for grace and mercy. Not everyone believed. Some hardened their hearts and clung to their traditions, laws, and idols. As soon as the Gospel was preached, lines were drawn. We don't know how many thousands of people were present, but 3,000 of them bravely came forward to be baptized (Acts 2:41). These new believers placed their faith in Jesus Christ as Lord and stepped out boldly to declare it to the world.

This was the moment when Christianity began, as a movement separate from Judaism. For these 3,000 believers, baptism was much more than just a ritual, an obligation, or quick bath. By being immersed in the water and rising out of it as a new creation, each believer was declaring to the world, "I am not who I was once was. I am no longer defined as a Jew or a Gentile. I am a Christian. I am no longer under the lordship of this world. I place myself under the lordship of Jesus Christ."

Imagine the murmurs of the skeptics. "Is that so and so? I can't believe they believe in this so-called Messiah." "Is that our son out there? What about our family's religious traditions?" "Is she really letting them dunk her in water? You've got to be kidding me."

Most likely, for some of those baptized that day, friendships were severed. Families turned their backs. By being baptized, these believers were rejecting the authority of Caesar (the Roman Emperor who declared himself to be a god) and were publically acknowledging the superior authority of Jesus Christ. In the months and years that followed, many of these 3,000 believers were threatened, treated as enemies of the state, persecuted, and even killed for their faith. But they had made the pledge. They had publically sealed their faith upon the water. There was no turning back.

Baptism is a big deal.

Why has baptism lost its significance in this day and age? Why do we treat it as a mere ritual? Why do so many new believers ask, "Do I really need to be baptized?" Why has baptism become a burden rather than a joy? Baptism is exciting, liberating, and commissioned.

The Representation of Baptism: Biblical baptism, as recorded in Scripture, is for the believer, and only the believer. Baptism is not Salvation, but is designed to proclaim Salvation. It's not something you do before you believe. It's something you do *because* you believe. Baptism is a serious decision that each individual believer must make. The word "baptism" is derived from the Greek root word *baptizo*, meaning "to submerge." Baptism is full immersion in water, symbolizing Christ's death, burial, and resurrection.

> *Or have you forgotten that when we were joined with Christ Jesus in baptism, we joined him in his death? For we **died** and were **buried** with Christ by baptism. And just as Christ was **raised** from the dead by the glorious power of the Father, now we also may live new lives. Since we have been united with him in his death, we will also be raised to life as he was.*
>
> *Romans 6:3-5*

Death: When you stand in the water to be baptized, you are publically professing your faith that Jesus Christ died for your sins. Simultaneously, you are declaring that your old, sinful life (before you knew Christ) is dead – nailed to the Cross.

Burial: When you are submerged under the water, you are publically acknowledging your faith that Jesus Christ was buried, and your old, sinful way of life is buried with him – never to rise again!

Resurrection: When you rise out of the water, you are declaring to the world your faith that Jesus Christ rose from the dead, giving you victory over sin and death. You are leaving your old life behind in the water and rising up as a new creation, empowered by the Holy Spirit to be the hands and feet of Christ in the world!

Baptism marks 360° of change. A full circle. You end up exactly where you started, but with a completely transformed life in Christ.

Baptism is all about newness of life. No matter what mistakes you made in the past, baptism marks a new beginning. It's more than just a clean slate. It's smashing your old slate entirely. It's more than just turning the page. It's getting a whole new book.

The Repentance of Baptism: Once, Jesus met a Samaritan woman standing by a well to draw water.

> *He had to go through Samaria on the way. Eventually he came to the Samaritan village of Sychar, near the field that Jacob gave to his son Joseph. Jacob's well was there; and Jesus, tired from the long walk, sat wearily beside the well about noontime. Soon a Samaritan woman came to*

> *draw water, and Jesus said to her, "Please give me a drink." He was alone at the time because his disciples had gone into the village to buy some food. The woman was surprised, for Jews refuse to have anything to do with Samaritans. She said to Jesus, "You are a Jew, and I am a Samaritan woman. Why are you asking me for a drink?" Jesus replied "If you only knew the gift God has for you and who you are speaking to, you would ask me, and I would give you living water." "But sir, you don't have a rope or a bucket," she said, "and this well is very deep. Where would you get this living water? And besides, do you think you're greater than our ancestor Jacob, who gave us this well? How can you offer better water than he and his sons and his animals enjoyed?" Jesus replied, "Anyone who drinks this water will soon become thirsty again.* ***But those who drink the water I give will never be thirsty again. It becomes a fresh, bubbling spring within them, giving them eternal life."***
>
> John 4:4-14

Although repentance has been defined in different ways, at the heart of repentance is the idea of "turning." Turning away from sin, and into righteousness. We try to make a 180° turn from sin, but we can't do it on our own. We strive, we struggle, we eventually manage a 45° turn, and we condemn ourselves for not being able to completely escape sin. We thirst for righteousness, but we're left thirsty.

At the center of the Great Commission you find a new disciple submerged in a tomb of water. The water in the picture of baptism is significant. Jesus said *"those who drink the water I give will never be thirsty again."*

Repentance is not "managing" our sin, blame-shifting our sin, or even confessing our sin. True repentance is impossible without God's grace. If we could make a 180° turn from sin by our own efforts, Jesus wouldn't have had to die.

The result of true repentance is being completely overwhelmed by grace. God transforms us from sinful to sanctified. We do turn from sin, but it is the Spirit working in us who helps us turn, empowering us to experience lifechange. When we fall, we fall into grace, not away from it. We thirst for righteousness, and God quenches that thirst with His mercy.

Repentance declares our desperate need for Jesus. Repentance is a sinner's guilty grief that reveals the reality of God's amazing grace.

Baptism represents the awesome power of God's love that saturates our lives. We are drenched in His redemption.

The Confirmation of Baptism: The Great Commission is designed to fully complete the Blueprint in the lives of those we are discipling. Disciples make disciples. We start with the command to go: "go and make disciples of all the nations." When a new believer accepts Jesus Christ as Lord and is baptized, it's time to move to the next phase of the Great Commission – the transition from "go" to "teach."

Teach: The Authorized Samurai

"The idea that this world is a playground instead of a battleground has now been accepted in practice by the vast majority of Christians."

A.W. Tozer

We are in a spiritual war between good and evil. The devil has no chance of winning the war, but he won't go down without a fight. The moment a new believer places their faith in Jesus Christ and declares it through baptism, Heaven rejoices and hell quakes. Satan will do everything in his power to stop you from teaching a new believer. From his perspective, the only thing worse than a new believer is one properly taught the Word of God and trained to teach others.

For we are not fighting against flesh-and-blood enemies, but against evil rulers and authorities of the unseen world, against mighty powers in this dark world, and against evil spirits in the heavenly places.

Ephesians 6:12

Teaching is not a job for the faint of heart. Teachers are fighting on the front lines of the battlefield. Not surprisingly, teaching is where many Christian casualties take place. Too often, new believers are left without proper instruction. Without someone to disciple them through the Christian walk, they are unable to make more disciples, and the multiplication process stops. This is exactly what the enemy wants.

Making disciples without teaching them is like enlisting men in the military and sending them into battle without weapons or armor.

The only thing worse than not having any teaching is having unbiblical teaching. Satan loves to introduce false teachings into the Church to confuse believers and cause division. Giving a believer false teaching is like sending a soldier onto the battlefield with defective equipment. The soldier thinks he's prepared to fight the enemy, but discovers at the worst possible moment that his gun won't fire and his armor won't stop a bullet.

The devil is relentless in his attacks. Biblical teaching is critically important for withstanding the enemy and gaining victory over him on the battlefield of everyday life.

The role of a teacher is *not* just for pastors, church leadership, Christian writers, or church-appointed "teachers." Every believer is commissioned by Jesus Christ to teach others. Teaching is for all believers, all the time. If we don't get serious about teaching, we're setting ourselves and others up for defeat.

The Samurai: You are an authorized teacher of the Word. Jesus said in Matthew 16:19,

> "And I will give you the **keys** of the Kingdom of Heaven. Whatever you **forbid** on earth will be forbidden in heaven, and whatever you **permit** on earth will be permitted in heaven."

We need to understand the magnitude of this passage or we will never grasp the awesome call we have to teach others. The Great Commission starts with these powerful words from Jesus Christ: *"I have been given all authority in heaven and on earth"* (Matthew 28:18). Jesus reminds His disciples of this to assure them that they've truly been commissioned. This is the same authority delivered in Matthew 16:19, your call to teach.

This verse is rooted in ancient Jewish tradition. In those days, boys would begin learning at the Temple from a very early age. Every few years, those who were struggling to learn the Scriptures would be sent away. Eventually, only a few young men remained. These top students had the opportunity to become apprentices of a rabbi. This was an honor and it took years of intense study of the Scriptures to get there. After years of learning from a rabbi, an apprentice could eventually become a rabbi himself – an authorized teacher.

When an apprentice became a rabbi, he would be given what were known as the "keys to the kingdom." When Jesus gave Peter the "keys to the Kingdom of Heaven," He was giving him the authority to teach, including the authority to "forbid and permit" and "bind and loose," which is the authority to interpret Scripture. In the Jewish culture of that day, a rabbi's authority to interpret Scripture was known as his "yoke."

> *Then Jesus said, "Come to me, all of you who are weary and carry heavy burdens, and I will give you rest. Take my yoke upon you. Let me teach you, because I am humble and gentle at heart, and you will find rest for your souls. For my yoke is easy to bear, and the burden I give you is light."*
>
> *Matthew 11:28-30*

Jesus Christ has commissioned you to share His yoke. You are called to study God's Word, open and close it, bind and loose it – and disciple others as a teacher of the Word.

You are an authorized teacher, a warrior on the front lines of a spiritual war. Like a samurai, you are charged by your master to live with honor and integrity, to train hard every day with intense discipline and self-sacrifice, to devote yourself wholeheartedly to prayer and the study of the Word, and to give everything you have in your spiritual warfare.

You are an authorized samurai.

The Sword: The Word of God is imperative to the care and protection of every believer. In the days of Paul's ministry, the Roman army was a powerful symbol of strength and victory. Paul uses the imagery of armor in Ephesians 6:10-18 to illustrate how we are to prepare and engage in spiritual battle:

> *A final word: Be strong in the Lord and in his mighty power. Put on all of God's armor so that you will be able to stand firm against all strategies of the devil. For we are not fighting against flesh-and-blood enemies, but against evil rulers and authorities of the unseen world, against mighty powers in this dark world, and against evil spirits in the heavenly places. Therefore, put on every piece of God's armor so you will be able to resist the enemy in the time of evil. Then after the battle you will still be standing firm. Stand your ground, putting on the belt of truth and the body armor of God's righteousness. For shoes, put on the peace that comes from the Good News so that you will be fully prepared. In addition to all of these, hold up the shield of faith to stop the fiery arrows of the devil. Put on salvation as your helmet, and* **take the sword of the Spirit, which is the word of God**. *Pray in the Spirit at all times and on every occasion. Stay alert and be persistent in your prayers for all believers everywhere.*

The sword is the only piece of equipment in this passage that is both defensive and offensive. While truth, righteousness, peace, faith, and Salvation are all necessities for every disciple, it is the Word that allows us to fight against the enemy. While the other pieces of armor defend us, the Word of God allows us to *advance forward* against the enemy. Are you ready to teach the Word?

> *We are human, but we don't wage war as humans do. We use God's mighty weapons, not worldly weapons, to knock down the strongholds of human reasoning and to destroy false arguments. We destroy every proud obstacle that keeps people from knowing God. We capture their rebellious thoughts and* **teach** *them to obey Christ.*
>
> 2 Corinthians 10:3-5

The End is the Beginning

"Don't let your hearts be troubled. Trust in God, and trust also in me. There is more than enough room in my Father's home. If this were not so, would I have told you that I am going to prepare a place for you? When everything is ready, I will come and get you, so that you will always be with me where I am."

John 14:1-3

Eternal life is the promise for all who place their faith in the Savior who gave Himself for us. He ascended into Heaven to prepare a place for us. When this life is over, the next thing you will know is the fullness of Christ's presence. Sin will no longer exist. The enemy will be destroyed forever. The days you spent separated from God by sin will be a distant memory - if remembered at all. Instead of being separated from God forever, *you will experience His presence forever.*

This was God's intention from the beginning! He is passionately pursuing His Creation, longing for an everlasting relationship with each and every one of us. It was never God's plan that anyone would perish and be separated from Him for eternity. And yet, that is precisely what Adam, Eve, and billions of people after them chose for themselves by rebelling against God through sin. Thousands of people die daily without ever knowing God or experiencing a relationship with Him.

God never wanted any of this to happen. Did God lose?

Here's the amazing thing: If you open your Bible to Revelation 21, you'll see that the end of history looks a lot like the beginning. In the end, everything will be restored to what God originally intended. In the last chapters of the Bible, we see Jesus Christ coming back to earth to rule as King. Every believer who has died will rise from the dead and join with the believers already living to meet Jesus Christ in the air. Paul describes this in 1 Corinthians 15:51-53,

But let me reveal to you a wonderful secret. We will not

> *all die, but we will all be transformed! It will happen in a moment, in the blink of an eye, when the last trumpet is blown. For when the trumpet sounds, those who have died will be raised to live forever. And we who are living will also be transformed. For our dying bodies must be transformed into bodies that will never die; our mortal bodies must be transformed into immortal bodies.*

Ultimately, this world will pass away, and a new Heaven and new Earth will be established as the ultimate consummation of all things. Revelation 21:4 promises this:

> *He will wipe every tear from their eyes, and there will be no more death or sorrow or crying or pain. All these things are gone forever.*

When that day comes, there will be "a loud shout from the throne, saying, 'Look, God's home is now among his people! He will live with them, and they will be his people'" (Revelation 21:3).

In the end, God will live in perfect, everlasting relationship with His people, walking and talking with them just like He did with Adam and Eve in the Garden. Even the animal kingdom will be restored to paradise:

> *In that day the wolf and the lamb will live together; the leopard will lie down with the baby goat. The calf and the yearling will be safe with the lion, and a little child will lead them all. The cow will graze near the bear. The cub and the calf will lie down together. The lion will eat hay like a cow. The baby will play safely near the hole of a cobra. Yes, a little child will put its hand in a nest of deadly snakes without harm. Nothing will hurt or destroy in all my holy mountain, for as the waters fill the sea, so the earth will be filled with people who know the LORD.*
>
> *Isaiah 11:6-9*

Consider that last part: "the earth will be filled with people who know the LORD."

In the end, there will no longer be a need for this book. No one will need to learn about God. We will all *know* God personally and fully, walking and talking with Him like you would with your best friend.

> *For as the waters fill the sea, the earth will be filled with an awareness of the glory of the LORD.*
>
> *Habakkuk 2:14*

In the end, God wins.

The only reason the world is so messed up right now is because we live in the transition time between sin infecting the world, and God restoring everything to perfection. The world may be evil now, but only for a moment. *Compared to eternity*, all of human history is like a fraction of a second.

Everything is about to be restored!

> *No eye has seen, no ear has heard, and no mind has imagined what God has prepared for those who love him.*
>
> *1 Corinthians 2:9*

Jesus Christ will perfect those things in your life the devil has been using to pull you down. The AUTHOR of your Salvation has full AUTHORity, and He will finish the work He started in you.

> *And I am certain that God, who began the good work within you, will continue his work until it is finally finished on the day when Christ Jesus returns.*
>
> *Philippians 1:6*

Imagine a place where sin is extinct and everyone around you is made perfect by the overwhelming presence of a Holy God. There will be no more harmful words, gossip, lust, deceit, anger, or jealousy. Perfection will be the new normal. What a day to rejoice!

Your war with that addiction – *Conquered!*

Your battle with being overweight – *Defeated!*

Your continual struggle with arthritis – *Left behind forever!*

The emotional scars of broken relationships – *Ancient history!*

The End is the Beginning. For the believer, the end of this temporary life on earth or the end of the world – whichever comes first – is the beginning of something infinitely better, infinitely more beautiful, and infinitely more valuable.

When John wrote the Book of Revelation by divine inspiration of God, he experienced a vision of what will happen at the end of the age – the stunning landscape of Heaven coming down to meet a new and perfect Earth as the New Jerusalem. He describes the indescribable with these words:

> *And the one sitting on the throne said, "Look, I am making everything new!" And then he said to me, "Write this down, for what I tell you is trustworthy and true." And he also said, "It is finished! I am the Alpha and the Omega—the Beginning and the End. To all who are thirsty I will give freely from the springs of the water of life. All who are victorious will inherit all these blessings, and I will be their God, and they will be my children. So he took me in the Spirit to a great, high mountain, and he showed me the holy city, Jerusalem, descending out of heaven from God. It shone with the glory of God and sparkled like a precious stone—like jasper as clear as crystal. The city wall was broad and high, with twelve gates guarded by twelve angels. And the names of the twelve tribes of Israel were written on the gates. There were three gates on each side—east, north, south, and west. The wall of the city had twelve foundation stones, and on them were written the names of the twelve apostles of the Lamb. The angel who talked to me held in his hand a gold measuring stick to measure the city, its gates, and its wall. When he measured it, he found it was a square, as wide as it was long. In fact, its length and width and height were each 1,400 miles. Then he measured the walls and found them to be 216 feet thick (according to the human standard used by the angel). The wall was made of jasper, and the city was pure gold,*

as clear as glass. The wall of the city was built on foundation stones inlaid with twelve precious stones: the first was jasper, the second sapphire, the third agate, the fourth emerald, the fifth onyx, the sixth carnelian, the seventh chrysolite, the eighth beryl, the ninth topaz, the tenth chrysoprase, the eleventh jacinth, the twelfth amethyst. The twelve gates were made of pearls—each gate from a single pearl! And the main street was pure gold, as clear as glass. I saw no temple in the city, for the Lord God Almighty and the Lamb are its temple. And the city has no need of sun or moon, for the glory of God illuminates the city, and the Lamb is its light. The nations will walk in its light, and the kings of the world will enter the city in all their glory. Its gates will never be closed at the end of day because there is no night there. And all the nations will bring their glory and honor into the city. Nothing evil will be allowed to enter, nor anyone who practices shameful idolatry and dishonesty—but only those whose names are written in the Lamb's Book of Life.

Revelation 21:5-27

Our earthly minds cannot begin to comprehend the riches of our Heavenly Father. We are heirs to an eternal fortune. Let me share some numbers with you about God's paving company in which you hold stock.

If you take the dimensions of the New Jerusalem – 1,400 miles cubed – we can calculate the cost of just *one* golden street running across the entire city.

A standard size bar of gold measures 7" x 3" x 2", weighs 400 ounces (27.5 lbs), and costs $640,000.

Let's assume the street is 15 feet wide, which is probably nowhere near as wide as it'll actually be. That's about 60 bars of gold wide.

If we take that street 1,400 miles long and multiply it by 5,280 ft per mile, we find out that the street is 7,392,000 feet long. That's equal to 12,672,000 bars laid end-to-end.

Multiply that by 60 bars for the width of the street, and you've got 760,320,000 bars of gold to pave *one* street. That's 304,128,000,000,000 ounces of gold.

These 760,320,000 bars, multiplied by the price of gold at $640,000 per bar, equals an astounding cost of $486,604,800,000,000 to pave just *one* street. That's 486 *trillion* dollars.

Do you realize how *wealthy* God is?

All of the gold that humans have mined over the last 200 years amounts to about ten billion ounces. That may sound like a lot, but compared to the 304 *trillion* ounces required to pave just *one* street, humans have only mined enough gold to pave $1/30,000^{th}$ of the street. At the rate we are currently mining, it will be six million years before we've mined enough gold to pave one street – assuming that much gold exists!

We're not going to pave this thing ourselves.

Heaven is so far beyond our imagination that we simply cannot comprehend how breathtaking it is.

C.S. Lewis put it simply: "Heaven is joy." Perhaps there is no better way to describe Heaven than joy. Absolute joy. Joy like we can't even imagine.

And Jesus said, "I am going to prepare a place for you."

The Architect's greatest work awaits us!

I don't know about you, but I want to make sure as many people get there as possible. Compared to eternity, nothing else seems to matter. The only alternative to Heaven is hell – eternal separation from God.

This world is about to pass away. Eternity is on the horizon. Too often, we live as if our lives here on earth are going to last forever. They're not. Sooner than we expect, we will all face eternity.

How will you spend eternity?

What about your family? How will they spend eternity? What about your friends? Your neighbors? Your coworkers? Your enemies?

It's urgent that we each become fully active in our faith and start doing something to help others find Salvation in Jesus Christ. Tomorrow is not guaranteed – **lifechange begins now.**

> *For God says, "At just the right time, I heard you. On the day of salvation, I helped you." Indeed, the "right time" is now. Today is the day of salvation.*
>
> *2 Corinthians 6:2*

The Blueprint isn't complete in your life until you've duplicated it in the life of another.

Go.

Baptize.

Teach.

Anything else we're doing is about us, and not about Jesus.

Thoughts from Chapter 9: The Great Commission

The Blueprint is not complete until it's been duplicated in the life of another. The Great Commission is Christ's final command before He ascended into Heaven. It starts with going into all the world to make disciples of all nations, including the people in your everyday life. Baptism is the next big step every Christian is called to take after Salvation. It symbolizes 360° of change – you end up exactly where you started, but with a completely transformed life in Christ. Teaching is not just for pastors or church-appointed "teachers." Every believer is called to teach. You are a supernatural samurai authorized to teach others the Word of God, which is the sword of the Spirit. Store up treasures in Heaven by investing in the only thing in this world with eternal value: people. Never assume that someone doesn't want Jesus. He died for the sins of all people, and He is preparing a place for us to spend eternity with Him. The only alternative is eternal separation from God. This world will soon be restored to the perfection God originally intended. Compared to eternity, nothing else seems to matter. Go. Baptize. Teach.

Questions to Consider

Are you storing up treasures on earth, or treasures in Heaven? What are some steps you can take to make a Heavenly deposit?

Have you ever felt ashamed to share your faith in Jesus Christ? What are some steps you can take to increase your Jesus swagger?

Have you ever said something that killed your testimony?

Is your spiritual walk covered with the dust of the Savior? What are some radical acts of kindness you can do to show others the love of Christ?

Have you ever assumed someone doesn't want to hear about Jesus? Why?

Have you been biblically baptized? If so, describe your experience. If not, are you ready to take that step?

Does the thought of teaching others God's Word intimidate you? What are some steps you can take to fully embrace the command to teach?

Have you ever made a disciple? Describe that experience.

Are you currently discipling someone? If so, how's it going? If not, who is God calling you to disciple?

What is your favorite part of Revelation 21?

If the world ended tomorrow, where would you spend eternity? What about your family? What about your friends?

Additional Verses to Study / How Can i Apply This?

- Romans 10:9-15

- 1 Peter 3:13-17

- 2 Peter 3:2-15

- Matthew 25:31-46

- 1 Thessalonians 4:13-18

- Hebrews 12:1-4

Building Blocks: Before i Move On...

☐ I am committed to the Great Commission.

☐ I am actively sharing my faith with the people in my life.

☐ I have been biblically baptized.

☐ I am teaching others the Word of God.

☐ I have made a disciple.

☐ I am continuing to duplicate the Blueprint in the lives of others.

Prayer

Heavenly Father, You are the Author of eternity and You hold time in Your hands. I praise You for giving me the glorious hope of an eternity spent with You. Please help me to live each day with eternity in mind. Open my eyes to the reality of the spiritual war happening around me. Give me the wisdom and strength to put on the full armor of God, stand firm in my faith, resist the devil, and send him fleeing. Give me the boldness to go into all the world and preach the gospel to all nations – beginning with those people I see in my daily life. Inspire me to teach Your Word with accuracy so everyone who hears will understand Your truths and apply Your Blueprint in their lives. Help me to be a disciple who makes disciples, duplicating Your Blueprint in the lives of others. Move me and lead me according to Your will, for Your glory. Amen.

Afterword

I am humbled and overwhelmed with praise. I feel truly blessed that God allowed me to play even a small role in building His Kingdom through the writing of this book. From the bottom of my heart, I want to thank you for joining me on this journey through nine chapters of intense Blueprinting.

Step by step, day by day, the walk of discipleship requires great faithfulness. It even means breaking the laws of physics and human understanding, embracing the supernatural. If you can explain all your ways, you aren't living in the fullness of an inexplicable God.

I want to encourage you to grow, be challenged, and continually search your heart, asking God to reveal new and powerful truths that will mold you into the worldchanger He is calling you to be.

When you see a picture of yourself, what do you see?

I hope you see someone who is forgiven, redeemed, a child of God, an ambassador of the Kingdom, and a disciple of Jesus.

I hope you see someone who is the light of the world, an eternal treasure of priceless value, commissioned to share Salvation with other jewels lost in a world of sin.

You are a picture of grace, framed in mercy.

You become a powerhouse of limitless ability when the God of power fills you without limitation.

Living by the Blueprint starts today.

> *For I can do everything through Christ, who gives me strength.*
>
> *Philippians 4:13*

You brought me this far
So why would I question You now?
You have provided
So why would I start to doubt?
I've never been stranded
Abandoned or left here to fight alone
So I'm giving You control

If peace is a river
Then let it sweep over me
I'm under fire
I know it's refining me
When I hear you calling out
I follow now wherever the road may go
I know you're leading me home

I lift my life up
I give it all in surrender
I lift my heart up
You can have it forever
All my dreams, all my plans
Lord, I leave it in your hands
I lift my life up
Have your way in me

  - Unspoken, "Lift My Life Up"

About the Co-Author
MATTHEW ELTON

Matthew Elton is Director of Media Ministry at Love City Fellowship in Gloversville, New York.

As a filmmaker, he is passionate about using the cinematic power of film and video to inspire others toward faith in Christ.

He graduated from Messiah College with a bachelor's degree in Film and Media Arts. He also happens to speak, read, and write basic Mandarin Chinese.

Matthew desires to radically follow Jesus Christ as Lord by living out the Sermon on the Mount and the Great Commission.

notes

notes

———————————— notes ————————————

notes

notes

notes

notes

notes

notes

notes

notes